A Steam Engine Pilgrimage

LOCHGIILPHEAD 24
Greenock
KINTYRE
ARRAN
Lochranza
Ayr

RAVENGLASS 23
WINDERMERE 22
Kendal
HAVERTHWAITE 21
Barrow in Furness
Lancaster
SETTLE
Harrogate
Blackpool
Keighley 15
HAWORTH 16
York
BURNLEY
Leeds
WIGAN 19
BOLTON 18
Liverpool
Manchester

Whitby
Scarborough
PICKERING 17

NORTH SEA

ISLE OF ANGLESEY
LLANBERIS 9
Blaenau Ffestiniog
PORTHMADOG 8
Harlech
Shrewsbury
TYWYN 7
CARDIGAN BAY
Bridgnorth
Ironbridge
BEWDLEY 11
Kidderminster
Market Bosworth
Coventry

Matlock Bath
CROMFORD 14
RAVENSHEAD 13
Nottingham
Derby

SHACKERSTONE 10
WANSFORD 12
Peterborough

THE WASH

Hereford
Gloucester
Chepstow
Newport
BRISTOL CHANNEL

ST MARY'S MILL 27
Swindon
Oxford
DIDCOT 1
London
KEW 2
Rochester
East Grinstead
TENTERDEN 4
SHEFFIELD PARK 6
HOVE 5
Lewes
Brighton
Rye

THAMES ESTUARY

MINEHEAD 26

ISLE OF WIGHT

DARTMOUTH (MARITIME) 3

ENGLISH CHANNEL

Railway
Steamship
Mill steam power
E Engineerium
or P Pumping
or R Steam Rally

SITES

1 Didcot, GWR Centre
2 Kew Bridge Engines, Kew
3 *Kingswear Castle,* Dartmouth
4 Kent and East Sussex Railway, Tenterden
5 British Engineerium, Hove
6 Bluebell Railway, Sheffield Park
7 Talyllyn Railway, Tywyn
8 Ffestiniog and Welsh Highland Railway, Porthmadog
9 Snowdon Mountain Railway, Llanberis
10 Battleship Line, Shackerstone
11 Severn Valley Railway, Bewdley
12 Nene Valley, Wansford
13 Papplewick Pumping Station, Ravenshead
14 Cromford

15 Settle
16 Keighley and Worth Valley Railway, Haworth
17 North Yorkshire Moors Railway, Pickering
18 Atlas Mills, Bolton
19 Wigan Pier
20 Queen Street Mill, Burnley
21 Lakeside and Haverthwaite Railway, Haverthwaite
22 Windermere Steamboat Museum
23 Ravenglass and Eskdale Railway, Ravenglass
24 *Vic 32,* Lochgilphead
25 Cadeby Light Railway, Cadeby
26 West Somerset Railway
27 St Mary's Mill

A Steam Engine Pilgrimage

Anthony Burton

PEN & SWORD
TRANSPORT

First published in Great Britain in 2017 by
Pen & Sword Transport
an imprint of
Pen & Sword Books Ltd
47 Church Street
Barnsley
South Yorkshire
S70 2AS

ISBN 978 1 47386 045 2

A CIP catalogue record for this book is available from the British Library

Typeset in Palatino by Mac Style Ltd, Bridlington, East Yorkshire
Printed and bound by Replika Press Pvt. Ltd.

Pen & Sword Books Ltd incorporates the imprints of Pen & Sword Archaeology, Atlas,
Aviation, Battleground, Discovery, Family History, History, Maritime, Military, Naval,
Politics, Railways, Select, Transport, True Crime, Fiction, Frontline Books,
Leo Cooper, Praetorian Press,
Seaforth Publishing and Wharncliffe.

For a complete list of Pen & Sword titles please contact
PEN & SWORD BOOKS LIMITED
47 Church Street, Barnsley, South Yorkshire, S70 2AS, England
E-mail: enquiries@pen-and-sword.co.uk
Website: www.pen-and-sword.co.uk

Contents

Preface

These journeys through the world of steam were made during the spring and summer of 1986. They were never intended to be comprehensive, could not be comprehensive, or I should be travelling still. Rather, they represent a personal selection of railways, boats and all things steaming that have given me special pleasure. The selection was also made to give at least an impression of the rich diversity of the subject. My steam journeyings began long before work started on this book and they will continue now that it is ended. This is a delectable slice from the middle of the steam pudding.

Anthony Burton

Preface to the Second Edition

Most of this book first appeared under the title *Steaming Through Britain* that was first published twenty or so years ago. The main text has been kept largely unchanged: after all, it represents the description of visits made at a particular time, but where necessary a few bits and pieces have been added as updates. I have, however, added some new sections, not in an attempt to make the book more comprehensive, but because they seemed to fill gaps that needed filling. I have added the chapter on replicas simply because my involvement with these machines proved to be immense good fun as well as being instructive. The fun element was also uppermost in my mind when writing about the lovely route to the sea, the West Somerset and added in a cruise past the site, down the Somerset coast – and the Welsh Highland is so much a part of the Ffestiniog system that I couldn't leave it out – in any case, how could a steam enthusiast resist the chance to visit a line with articulated Garratts. I hope readers will excuse me for adding one non-steaming steam engine.

Chapter 1

Waiting for the Train

Each summer, birds sing, flowers bloom and large numbers of men, and rather fewer women, clamber into boilersuits to shovel coal, to grease and clean machinery and to coax back into panting life engines which, by all the laws of logic, should have been consigned to the scrap heap. Several, indeed, have been sent for scrap only to be hauled out again and, with infinite labour, restored to their former glories. The steam enthusiasts are at work. Locomotives emerge from winter hibernation in their engine sheds. Traction engines lumber down country lanes, queues of motorists, frustrated or enchanted, behind them. Great beam engines nod their ponderous heads.

What is the appeal of steam? Why should so much love and affection be lavished on mere mechanical objects? The answers to these questions will, I hope, emerge during this description of a steam pilgrimage. There are those whose enthusiasm extends no further than one engine or, at most, one particular group of engines: the steam locomotive buffs, the beam engine enthusiasts, the potterers in steam launches. Others make no such distinction and need only a whiff of that heady mixture of smoke and hot oil to send them into ecstatic reveries. I count myself among their number. So, in these journeys, we shall meet engines of every kind and variety – but where does one start? Well, it seems a good idea to remind ourselves that the steam engine, now a rare and exotic creature, was once the common workhorse of Britain, and what could be more mundane a setting than the morning commuter train to London?

The 9.20 am from Didcot to Paddington attracts a large number of travellers; not because it is especially fast, for it is not, and certainly not for the standards of comfort on offer. The carriages are of what one might describe as 'a certain age', and the characteristic sound they emit is a high-pitched twang as the aged springs respond to the arrival of a commuter bottom. Its main attraction is the price of the ticket, for this is the first train of the morning on which a cheap day-return is available. So when I have to visit London this is the train for me. I join other parsimonious passengers in the vast car park which, until recently, had the appearance of a battlefield after a heavy bombardment, for the whole surface was scarred and pitted with holes full of dark, oily water. It was not a sight to gladden the heart. But occasionally, just occasionally, I look across from the footbridge over the lines, over the trucks and wagons, to where a thin wisp of smoke rises up from a copper-capped chimney above a dark green boiler. Then Didcot does not mean British Rail 125s dashing off to Swindon and my morning train to Paddington, because the smoke that drifts across the lines carries something other than the smell of a steam locomotive – it brings the scent of nostalgia. In imagination one could leave BR to the present and turn back to the days of the Great Western Railway (GWR). Didcot Railway Centre has opened its doors for a journey into the past.

There are some centres and preserved lines whose main ambition is to re-create the pleasure of travel by steam railway, but this is not the principal aim at Didcot. Here they want to re-create the essence of the old GWR, probably the best loved railway in the world. And if you start as I did with a visit to the museum building, refusing to be side-tracked by the allures of gentle simmerings or the call to action of the steam whistle, you will discover something of the individual character of this special railway. You may not discover what made the Western Railway Great, but you will find something to suggest why so many accept the description. The GWR was adept at public relations long before British Rail came along with its strange slogans – 'This is the Age of the Train', as though the railways were a new invention or, worse, 'We're Getting There'. Yes, you long to say, but will you ever arrive?

The GWR promoters invested their railway with glamour, and they started as early as the 1890s. There was the promise of seaside holidays, touched with something more exotically European if you boarded the Cornish Riviera Express. That was followed by 'The World's Fastest Train' – the Cheltenham Flyer. The railway was 'merchandised' before anyone had even heard the word: you could buy Great Western jigsaws; you could choose your holidays from *Holiday Haunts* which, needless to say, publicised only those attractive locations to be reached by the one railway; and rail enthusiasts could read *The Great Western Magazine.* It was the railway, above all others, which set out to fix an image in the public mind; just how well it succeeded can be judged from the vast array of GWR devotees who remain faithful long after its demise.

It started with an advantage, of course, for it was a line begun with reckless boldness by the most exciting engineer of the nineteenth century, Isambard Kingdom Brunel. Change came, more dramatically here perhaps than on any other line, but the imprint of the little man with the tall hat and the big cigar lingers still over all things Great Western. The GWR *was* unique: all the publicists had to do was make sure the world was aware of its uniqueness. That is the message Didcot still sends out today – and it does so by presenting the railway in historical perspective.

Didcot is a big site and it is easy to ramble around picking up fragments of the story where they lie – carriages awaiting restoration here, old station signs there, and afterwards a glimpse in the shed of dismembered locomotives. I rather enjoy such aimless meanderings, but I will bring a little order to the proceedings by going back to the beginnings of the Great Western.

Brunel was a man with breadth of vision: where lesser mortals were content to set rails 4 feet 8½ inches apart, for no better reason than that was the gauge of the colliery line where George Stephenson went to work on his steam locomotive, Brunel set out to discover what would be the best gauge for a railway. Width, he decided, was indeed the thing; a broad seven-foot gauge to provide an even ride at high speed, and the Great Western was built to that gauge. Whatever its virtues, the broad gauge suffered from one fatal disadvantage: too much money had been invested in what was being called the standard gauge. On 20 April 1892, the last of the broad gauge was removed. But at Didcot it has been revived and we can all stand and stare at the wide tracks and think what might have been.

In 1985, on the 150th anniversary of the GWR, a replica of one of the most famous of the old broad-gauge locomotives, *The Iron Duke,* arrived at Didcot. It came on a long, low truck and there, alas, it stayed. There was no suitable crane to lift it, and no one would lend a crane, without the exchange of a great deal of folding currency. The great anniversary came and went and *The Iron Duke* sulked on a siding like Achilles in his tent, unable to join the rest of the army of locomotives. The following year, however, all that changed and *The Iron Duke* charged up and down a short length of broad-gauge track in triumphal style. Today the locomotive no longer steams, but even as a static exhibit the old engine is still redolent of the great days of the

The replica of Daniel Gooch's *Iron Duke* in its new home at the National Railway Museum, York. (Richard Kelly)

GWR and now has a new home at the National Railway Museum in York. There is, however, another replica of the broad gauge days, a Firefly class locomotive that is steamed on special occasions. And alongside the broad track is a reminder that not everything Brunel did was a huge success. There is a length of tubing from the ill-fated atmospheric railway that, for a brief period, extended the route westward from Exeter.

A visit from a broad-gauge locomotive is a rare event at Didcot, but the slimmer engines are regularly on display. With luck, the enthusiast can see the names that helped make the GWR famous – the Halls, the Castles, and the Kings, regal names for regal locomotives. But there is little room for steaming here, so one has the sensation of seeing a caged animal, like a great, sleek cat at a zoo. The tiger may be snoozing, the panther padding its confined home, but the watcher is never in doubt of the contained power waiting to be released. Just occasionally, that steam power is let out as the engines head excursion trains to various parts of the country, but of that more later.

At Didcot, the visitor can poke and pry, and see something of the work going on in the sheds. A stripped-down locomotive is not always the loveliest of beasts. Rusty iron, dull steel and greasy brass are not appealing, and rivets and stays, while they have their admirers, are not noted for their beauty. Yet, given time, patience, money and a great deal of work, the most unpromising of raw material is transformed. A splendidly colourful butterfly will emerge from the dull chrysalis. It is not the speediest work. One old engine was brought in to have a little work done to the springs, and it seemed sensible while it was there to have a go at the boiler, and then the valves, and so it has been going on for the last ten years. But no one minds very much. It is, after all, a labour of love.

Memories of broad gauge days: old GWR disc signals at Didcot. (Anthony Burton)

There are only a few permanent staff at Didcot, but the Great Western Society has over 4,000 members, and they can rely on getting a couple of hundred to help out when required. There are glamorous jobs, less glamorous jobs and a lot of hard, dirty jobs as well. Some of the

hardest work goes on in the workshops and I always enjoy a visit there. There is something awesome about the scale of these steam monsters, and the power they represent. There is tremendous satisfaction too in seeing a handsome carriage emerge from the bits and pieces that were once a farmer's henhouse, or a fine locomotive steam again when it had seemed destined for the cutting torch of the scrapyard. Look, for example, at the finest Didcot has to offer – *Drysllwyn Castle*. It could not be anything but GWR: the distinctive shape of the tapered boiler, the familiar green, the gleaming copper of the chimney and the promise of speed in the six big driving wheels. Here you see elegance and power in splendid partnership, the essence of the Great Western Railway.

At Didcot there is still enough space to display engines and carriages to advantage, and to feature other aspects of the railway scene, from the strange disc signals of the Brunel era to a demonstration of how to collect a mailbag on a moving train. It is all there to be picked over at leisure – the GWR on display like a composite picture. Many of the elements I enjoy can be found here, but it by no means represents the complete railway story, and certainly not the whole story of steam. The Great Western Railway may have a grand history, but the age of steam was a century old when the first locomotive rolled out on to Brunel's broad-gauge tracks. In my travels in search of steam I found myself hopping through time as well as trundling through the country. No two places were ever the same: diversity rules, thank heavens. Perhaps just one theme ran through every journey I made. Whenever I saw living steam, I found people who had worked with love, and generally for love, to bring that world of steam to life.

Chapter 2

Pumps and Paddles

This is the first half of a circular journey – geographically and chronologically – from London around the south-east, and from the start of the steam story to the last stage of steam railway development. The beginning of the story was not in the world of transport, but in the need for mines to pump water from great depths, and it began as far back as the end of the seventeenth century.

Thomas Savery received a patent for a 'New Invention for raising of water … by the impellant force of Fire' in 1698, and he manufactured this machine at a workshop near the Thames in London. The building has long gone and the site is now a playground, with not even a plaque to mark where the steam age was born. Not that Savery's engine was especially successful; nor was it very like subsequent engines. It worked by using the pressure of steam to force water up from the bottom of the mine. This meant setting a boiler below ground. The engine was referred to by Savery as 'The Miner's Friend', but as the colliers watched Savery's giant kettle being installed and a fire lit beneath it, they must have felt that with friends like that they had no need of enemies. Open fires and explosive gases are not generally felt to be compatible with the highest standards of safety.

Savery's engine may not have been the perfect answer to the problem of

A railway rarity: a GWR steam railcar at Didcot. (Great Western Society)

removing water from mines, but it set others thinking about the possibilities of using steam, among them Thomas Newcomen. His pumping engine was gloriously simple in concept. Take a large open-topped cylinder and put a piston in it. Let steam into the space below the piston, forcing the air out until the whole chamber is filled with steam, then spray cold water on to the cylinder. The steam will condense, creating a vacuum, and air pressure will force the piston into the cylinder. To make a pumping engine, all you have to do is hang the piston rod off one end of a beam pivoted at the centre and hang pump rods from the opposite end of the beam. Without steam, the weight of the pump rods would naturally pull the beam down in that direction, but with this process the piston can be forced down, pulling the pump rods up. Endlessly repeating the process causes the beam to sway to and fro and the pump to move up and down steadily.

The Newcomen engine worked, and soon massive beam engines began to appear at Britain's collieries. Unfortunately, vast quantities of coal were needed to fire the boilers. This was not a problem at a colliery, where you have coal in plenty, but things were different in the case of the metal mines – particularly the tin and copper mines of Devon and

Cornwall, where coal was scarce and expensive. There was a need for a better, more economical machine, a need which was met by our third engineering hero, Mr James Watt.

Watt has been called the father of the steam engine, but so has Thomas Newcomen and so, if rather less frequently, has Thomas Savery. Whether any of them deserves the title, I shall leave the reader to decide. But what was the contribution that gave James Watt his popular claim to the title? Forget all the storybook images of a young lad watching a kettle boiling over and shouting *Eureka*, or the Scots equivalent, and dashing off to invent the steam engine. Reality is less romantic.

The young engineer was, in fact, pondering the practical problem of the inefficiency of the Newcomen engine when he identified the source of the difficulty. Huge amounts of energy were being wasted in heating the cylinder after each stroke, when it had just been doused in a cold spray. In a flash of inspiration he hit on one of those gloriously simple ideas that can change the world. Condensing steam was fine, but why do it in the cylinder? The steam could be condensed in a separate chamber connected to the cylinder; the effect would be the same, but the cylinder could still be kept hot. Having realised that this was part of the answer, he saw the other element of the problem. Heat was being wasted because the cylinder was open to the air. But close the cylinder and air pressure cannot act on the piston. So, said Mr Watt, why use air pressure at all? What is wrong with steam pressure? On one side of the piston you can still create a vacuum, and on the other you can provide the drive by means of steam under pressure. What is more, you no longer need pump rods to hang at one end of the beam, you need only provide steam pressure on alternate sides to make your piston go backwards and forwards. Attach that moving piston rod to a crank and you have the means to turn a wheel.

The replica *Firefly* at Didcot. (Great Western Society)

This was the basis of movement in paddle steamer and screw steamer, steam locomotive and traction engine. But the beam engine with its pump rods on one end and its cylinder and piston on the other, which started the whole thing, was to be just as important and still remains in everyday use as a working machine right up to the present day. Over the years the engines were to get ever bigger, ever more powerful, reaching an apotheosis in that great symbol of Victorian civic improvement: the waterworks supplying the needs of towns and cities. And nowhere in Britain will you see mightier engines than at Kew Pumping Station where, after this long introduction, we begin our travels.

Kew Pumping Station is not difficult to find. It stands near the northern end

The immense chimney of the former Kew pumping station dominates this part of the West London skyline. (London Museum of Water and Steam)

of Kew Bridge, and the tall boiler-house chimney is still one of the dominant features of this area of London. It is not the size alone that impresses; it has a style that pleases, the more so perhaps because one does not think of steam engine chimneys as being beautiful; useful certainly, but not noted for elegance. But to the Victorians, the new pumping station was more than a building to house machinery; it was a matter for local pride. The arrival of this new installation meant that decent standards of health and hygiene were available to the householders of London: turn a tap and, as if by miracle, pure, clear water would emerge. The age of taking dirty germ-ridden flows from the Thames had ended. In the mid-nineteenth century the river was so filthy that the curtains in the Houses of Parliament were soaked in disinfectant daily to protect the delicate nostrils of the Honourable Members – and the, no doubt, even more delicately

patrician senses of their Lordships – from what became known as 'The Great Stink'. At Kew, water was to be pumped to filter beds by the power of steam, for the good of all. So the first glimpse that you get of the station is a statement in one of the approved styles for civic dignity, in this case Italianate, that we are in the presence of mighty works. Today, that same tall chimney is a signpost pointing down to the biggest working engine in Britain, a lure for me and for other steam enthusiasts who hurry along to the base of the chimney and the engine house itself. Once inside, one can only stand and wonder.

Kew Pumping Station is not just a simple building with an engine chuffing away inside. It started out on a comparatively small scale, but success built on success: more water was required, more power needed and more engines were added. They worked away, unnoticed by the world at large, until

A general view of the main display area at Kew, which is dominated by the imposing triple-expansion engine at the centre of the picture. (London Museum of Water and Steam)

in 1944 they suffered the fate that was to befall all the great pumping engines: compact electrical pumps took over from the steam giants. Now they have been preserved, restored and joined by a number of smaller brethren specially brought in to turn Kew into 'a living steam museum'. To come to Kew is to see the steam engine at its most majestic, for you will see no bigger anywhere in Britain. The size is impressive enough, goodness knows, but with it goes a sense of serenity, of total control and elegance of movement – elegance in the sense that mathematicians use the word to describe a problem solved with ingenuity and a minimum of complexity. It makes little difference whether you have ever seen a steam engine before, or whether you know how it works, for it is possible to appreciate these great machines simply as objects of beauty. Apart from the sheer scale, it is the perfection of movement, of shining metal bars sliding one against the other or tracing arabesques in the air, that makes the lasting impression. I shall try to give the reader some idea of this purity of movement in a moment, but first the history books will help put these machines into perspective.

We left our steam engine story with James Watt. He was a fortunate man in that, unlike so many inventors, he was able to profit from his own work. He went into partnership with a successful entrepreneur and manufacturer, Matthew Boulton, and they acquired a virtual monopoly of steam engine construction throughout the latter part of the eighteenth century. Watt was like many another, however, in that having made his initial grand advance he was reluctant to take any further steps forward. As far as James Watt was concerned, the steam engine had reached a peak of perfection and, protected by all-embracing patents, he made sure that no one else had the chance to try for better things. This was irritating, especially for the engineers of Cornwall who, more than anyone else,

had an incentive, in the form of high fuel costs, to look for improvements. Their chance came when the clock struck midnight at the end of more than a day or even a year, and the eighteenth century gave way to the nineteenth. James Watt's patents ran out. The Cornishmen rushed to try out their new ideas, and a second golden age of steam was born. Just how successful the Cornishmen were can be seen at Kew.

There are two ways to make a steam engine do more work: increase its size or increase the pressure of the steam. Watt was a low-pressure steam man. The Cornish engineers, who included such redoubtable figures as Richard Trevithick, favoured higher pressures. Then, as demand increased, they set to work improving the pumps, improving the engines, and going for bigger and more powerful machines. New engine works were set up, the two most famous being on the Cornish north coast at Hayle: the Copperhouse Foundry and Harveys. Two of the steam monsters of that period, one from each manufacturer, can be seen here in Kew. We are all accustomed now to the notion of engine cylinders. We have them in our cars, rows of them, the little pistons bobbing up and down at great speed. You could drop the cylinder block from the largest car into one of the Kew engine cylinders and scarcely notice it was there. The earlier of the two, supplied by Copperhouse, was built in 1845. The cylinder is 90 inches in diameter, while the Harvey engine which joined it in 1869 is 100 inches across. The Harvey piston moves up and down for a full 11 feet at each stroke, and this giant among engines could shift 10 million gallons of water a day from the Thames to the householders of West London. The statistics are impressive enough, but they cannot prepare you for the sight of the engines *in situ,* or for the sight of the 90 inch, which is still regularly steamed.

The first surprise is the quietness of the engine room; no clatter or racket,

The Boulton and Watt engine at Kew. (London Museum of Water and Steam)

to be reconciled, a circle to be squared. The piston rod must move in a straight line, travelling vertically up and down in the cylinder, but the swinging beam which carries it carves the arc of a circle in the air. The engineer who performed the miracle of squaring the circle was, once again, James Watt. He arranged a shifting parallelogram of metal rods and hung his piston from one corner. It is known as Watt's parallel linkage, but the bald description gives no idea of the beauty of the device at work. The rods shift and slide, solid metal chunks gleaming with reddish-brown oil, moving as gently and smoothly as a silk scarf in a breeze. And here you come to the heart of one of the appeals of steam: a natural force of great power controlled by machines which manage to be at once massive and effortlessly fluent in their motion. Everything is there for you to see, not tucked away but asking to be admired. Everything takes its time from the rhythmic motion of the overhead beam: simple, mechanical linkages take their timing from the nodding steel to open and close the valves which maintain the steady motion. The wisps of steam are the only signs of the power locked up in the tons of moving parts.

You can see other engines here at Kew – a Boulton and Watt of 1820, a fine triple expansion and more – a hall full of them, all nodding and bowing to one another in a stately steam quadrille; but it is the giant engine that draws visitors back again and again. Sometimes I just stand and admire the beauty of its motion, sometimes I ponder over the men who conceived and built such a machine, and occasionally I remember that it was part of a mundane system doing nothing more romantic than ensuring that when you turned a tap in Brentford water came out of it. You need that sort of thought to stop yourself being carried away by fanciful notions.

The setting is undeniably romantic, designed to impress, but what mattered was how well the engines worked, and

just a gentle sighing and a rumble as if a giant were turning in his sleep in some subterranean cavern. There is no sense of haste; the atmosphere is almost churchlike, heightened by the design, with tall fluted columns supporting and containing the moving engine. High above, the iron beam slowly rocks; a worryingly lightweight affair it was thought at the time, a mere 24 tons, so it was strengthened later just to be on the safe side. From the end of the beam hangs the piston rod – but not quite directly.

There are two apparent irreconcilables

what the balance sheet looked like at the end of the day. Well, the 90-inch engine cost £6,360 new and, since it did its job for just short of a century, I do not think the waterworks' managers could complain about poor returns. Harveys also provided an engine man and assistant to make sure everything went well, and they cost 13 shillings and 6 pence (67 new pence) per pair per day. Today, the engine man setting everything in motion for the delight of visitors is likely to be a volunteer working for nought shillings nought pence per day.

It is difficult to think of the Kew engines as having a part to play in the transport revolution. You cannot visualise one of them, the size of a moderate semi, trundling off on its own down the road. But go to the engine hall and look at the small rotative beam engine, with its spinning flywheel, and you realise how men's minds began to work 200 years ago. With quite a small cylinder, but using high-pressure steam, you could get a lot of work from the engine, and if the engine could turn a wheel it could make something move. Trevithick made valiant attempts to interest the world in his steam locomotive, but with little success. The story was rather different on the water. The paddle steamer was at work successfully long before the first commercial railway was established. So my next logical step was to leave Kew, cross the river and head south-east for the Medway in search of steam on the water.

Britain's first paddle steamer appeared in 1788, some time after successful experiments in France and America. For the next half-century steam on the water meant the paddle steamer, but then came the screw propeller and the role of the paddler was diminished. However, it remained the favourite of the excursion trade. No self-respecting seaside resort was complete without its paddle steamer at the end of the pier, offering trips along the coast, around the lighthouse or up the estuary. Among the trips designed to show the delights of river scenery, none could offer more than those along the River Dart. The first River Dart Steamboat Company was formed in 1836, and in 1877 a new company took over and began the construction of the Castle line of steamers. Three vessels were built in the first batch and expanding trade called for an addition to the fleet, which arrived in 1904 – *Kingswear Castle*. The paddle steamer's manoeuvrability made it the first choice for the winding river so, when *Kingswear Castle* showed signs of ageing, a replacement was ordered. But, although the hull was battered and bent, the engine was still turning merrily, so the management put it into the new vessel. The second *Kingswear Castle* took to the water with a 1924 hull concealing a 1904 engine. This was the vessel I was to join on a blustery summer day on the Medway.

I was waiting for *Kingswear Castle* at Strood pier, not the world's most romantic spot. To one side a crane was picking up scrap iron by magnet, collecting the hunks from one pile and dropping them with a clatter and a rusty cloud on another pile. Downstream, the wharf was empty, but moored out on the river was a spritsail barge – a happy reminder of days when I sailed these grand old vessels on this same water. The only human activity was from a pair of fishermen in a small boat, hauling in nets without much success. It was not a cheerful scene, and a strong east wind did little to help. A train rumbled across the bridge past Rochester Castle, but nothing else moved. Then a pennant showed above the buildings on the opposite bank and around the corner came a vessel with the unmistakable shape of a paddle steamer.

Paddle steamers, however lean and sleek their hulls appear when viewed from the side, always have a pronounced midriff bulge, so they present a quite different view seen from ahead. The side view of *Kingswear Castle* is the very picture of Victorian elegance for, although built in the 1920s, she has retained the styling of her class. The hull is long and low, with a single funnel set behind the little wheelhouse on the bridge. Seen straight on, however, she is almost dumpy. A glance at her measurements shows why: the basic hull is 113 feet 8 inches overall, with a 17-foot 6-inch beam, but the paddle boxes covering the wheels extend the width at that point to 28 feet. There was time to take in both aspects as she swung around in a wide curve, her twin wakes creaming the water until she arrived with a minimum of fuss and bother beside the pier. It looks effortless, but anyone who has handled a large vessel will know it is not that simple. Manoeuvring usually

The paddle steamer *Kingswear Castle* back in her home waters on the River Dart at Dartmouth. (Paddle Steamer Kingswear Castle Trust)

involves lines being thrown ashore and attached to pivotal points to simplify the process. *Kingswear Castle* carries a small crew and there was no one on shore to take lines, other than passengers. So the captain, John Megoran, has to bring his ship precisely alongside, so that a deckhand can reach across and slip a line over a bollard. It is not a steering exercise I should care to try without a great deal of practice, but it was achieved perfectly, the gangplank went out, and I and a coachload of other passengers went on board.

The first thing that strikes you about the vessel is its immaculate condition. Woodwork gleams, brasses shine – the latter as much a matter of necessity as of

pride, for without regular cleaning the metalwork would soon be corroded by salt spray. Elsewhere, pride shows in the attractively-painted paddle boxes with a representation of the castle in the centre, and in the head decoration, the elaborate scroll work on the bows. This effect has not been easily achieved. *Kingswear Castle* went out of service in 1965 and was purchased by the Paddle Steamer Preservation Society two years later. For three years she was berthed on the Isle of Wight, but work was so slow that, rather than restoration going forward, deterioration was actually setting in. The decision was taken to move her to the Medway where work could be carried out more easily if only because more hands were available.

It was to prove a long and costly process, involving replacement of the paddle wheels, a vast amount of refurbishment of decks and paintwork, rebuilding of the wheelhouse; to the patient volunteers the list must have seemed endless. There was an end, however. In November 1983 she was put through her trials and passed them, literally with flying colours. And today she takes passengers for river outings just as she did sixty years ago, with the engine turning over as quietly and efficiently as it did more than eighty years ago. It is a story not dissimilar to that of Kew: the past is brought to life by the work of the unpaid; unpaid, that is, in cash terms, but how do you put a value on the knowledge that you have helped to put such a vessel back on the water?

The first attraction to the steam enthusiast is inevitably the engine room. A beguiling glimpse of moving machinery can be had through a grille in front of the wheelhouse; a crank turning over slowly to drive the paddle wheels that slap the water on either side. Down below, the engine is revealed, but it is less immediately obvious than the boiler. The firedoors open to display a long firebox full of glowing coals. There is more to

keeping a boiler going than just chucking in a few shovelfuls of coal. The fire needs to be evenly, but quite thinly, spread. The golden rule for adding coal is 'little and often', but the vital thing is that the coal must be added to the right part of the fire. Firing a boiler is a skilled job, not easily learned, and the objective is to provide the right amount of steam, which in this case means a working pressure of 120 psi (pounds per square inch). Britain may have gone metric, but in the world of steam imperial measurements still rule.

The engine room is a warm, cosy spot when a chill wind is whistling down the Medway. There is plenty of space around the front of the boiler to take coal from either of the bunkers, one to each side of the vessel. The engineer here was blessed by having them filled with good Welsh steam coal; only those who have tried to keep a steady reading on a pressure gauge while firing with inferior coal will know what a blessing that is.

Then there is the engine itself. As at Kew, it has a beautiful simplicity. The steam at its steady 120 psi passes into a horizontal cylinder a mere 13 inches in diameter, almost a miniature after the 100-inch at Kew. Essentially, however, the work is the same, except that instead of pushing at the end of a beam the piston turns a crankshaft. There is one other difference: the exhaust steam is still under pressure, so instead of being wasted it is fed into a second cylinder. As the steam pressure has been reduced in passing through the first cylinder, it needs to act on a greater area, so this is a 25-inch-diameter cylinder. There is one further refinement to be added. As in James Watt's eighteenth-century engine, the steam is finally condensed in a separate condenser, and that condensed steam can be fed back to the boiler.

There is a sense of rightness about such an engine, a most satisfying feeling of completeness; nothing is wasted, everything is put to use and all the mechanisms are on show. Pumps and valves work through simple linkages and all are accessible for the regular round with the oil can. There is another special thrill about this engine room, for what you are seeing is the heart of the last coal-fired paddle steamer at work in Britain. It is not the last paddle steamer, because the Society owns a second, larger and rather grander vessel, the *Waverley,* which can also claim uniqueness – *Waverley* is the last sea-going paddle steamer in the world. Every year these two historic craft rendezvous in the Medway, to double up, if such a thing is possible, on uniqueness.

By now, the reader may be wishing to paraphrase the reporter interviewing Mrs Abraham Lincoln after the assassination of her husband, and ask: 'But did you enjoy the trip, Mr Burton?' Truth to tell, I saw little of the outside world for a long while, so engrossed was I in the engine room. But I did emerge eventually and, yes, I did enjoy the trip. Several of the most interesting sights had already slid away astern, and the way ahead was dominated by two themes: pleasure boats and power stations.

The boats at their moorings, ranging in size from dinghies to ocean-going yachts, are lined up by the tide to parade-ground precision. Metal guys twang and slap against alloy masts in the hubbub, which is now the mark of the sailing club or marina, but among them you can still spot the occasional working boat. A pair of oyster smacks lay side by side and, as we approached the Isle of Grain, the sailing barge *Cabby* slipped out from behind the headland. This is one of the great sights of the south-east coast, though *Cabby* was taking no chances in the strong wind. A foresail was filled with the stiff breeze but her mainsail was brailed, pulled in and tied to the mast. With canvas reduced to a minimum, she was still a bonny vessel, and historic barge and historic steamer exchanged salutations as they passed on the river. Even today, the Medway is not entirely given over to pleasure boats. The tall stack of the power station dominates the horizon and down by the jetty one

of the new generation of big colliers was unloading. Giant grabs dipped greedily into the hold and came up with their jaws full of coal. Beyond that one could see the second chimney of the second power station.

We turned for home and ahead of us a brightly coloured sail zoomed across the water. A windsurfer flashed past; his body almost horizontal except when the board hit a particularly high crest and bounced in the air, flying an incredible distance before landing and continuing on its way. The windsurfer turned and made a run across *Kingswear Castle's* bows which showed remarkable confidence or considerable stupidity, for had he hit us we would have been searching our wake for the pieces. I must confess to preferring *Cabby's* stately progress to that technicolour dashing backwards and forwards across the estuary, but he was soon left behind.

The Medway has always been an important route from the sea and one that needed to be defended, a point somewhat humiliatingly brought home in 1667 when the Dutch fleet sailed up the Thames, captured Sheerness and continued on to Chatham where they attacked the English fleet, destroying five ships and capturing others. It was not one of the great episodes of English naval history, but there is evidence in plenty that over the centuries defence has been taken seriously. Forts dot the shoreline and, most spectacu-larly, Upnor Castle looms above the water and the village of Upper Upnor. This is one of the loveliest and most fascinating spots along the river, because it offers such remarkable contrasts. The road runs right down to the water's edge and ends on one side with the tall, imposing walls of the castle, and across the street with an extravagant little gazebo at the end of the garden of a fine country house. From here the road rises steeply between weatherboard cottages and past the Tudor Rose, a pub of great character and good ale. What more could one ask?

The climax of the journey was the arrival at the pier which stands beside what was, until recently, the Royal Dockyard of Chatham, established under the rule of two monarchs – Henry VIII and Elizabeth I – who, if they differed in many ways, agreed about the importance of the Navy. It still looks quite splendid with its workshops and warehouses ranged down by the riverfront, but the yards have now closed, and its only future is as yet another tourist attraction. Chatham withstood wars and bombardment, but fell to the accountant's pen. The figures were displayed to demonstrate the rightness of the decision for closure, but some details were absent: tradition, no price fixed; skills acquired over centuries do not show up on the computer.

So Chatham will be preserved after a fashion, though much of the life has gone from it. At least *Kingswear Castle* still lives, still plies the trade for which she was built. By the pier I saw two more candidates for resurrection – two steam tugs, one with conventional screw propeller and the other a paddle tug. I wished the restorers well as *Kingswear Castle* swung away to head back across the river to Strood.

Since writing those words, the site has reopened as Chatham Historic Dockyard. One can still regret the loss of a real working life, but if that had to go at least it is being remembered in a wholly appropriate way that does justice to the past. It's a success – and there's even something new for the steam enthusiast. Among the preserved warships is the Royal Navy sloop HMS *Gannet*, built in 1878, which could either be worked under sail or using the two-cylinder compound steam engine. It is tempting to think that when steam came in, sail was immediately redundant. Of course, this was never true but it is interesting to note that according to statistics, the vessel had a top speed of 12½ knots under steam power but could manage a sprightly 15 knots under sail.

There has been one further change. *Kingswear Castle* has come back to home waters, once again plying the waters of the River Dart and steaming past the castle that gave her a name. The vessel also has a brand new boiler and it was only after I heard about that, and was told about the old one that was being jettisoned, that I discovered something I wish I'd known when I first went aboard. That original boiler was built by Riley Brothers of Stockton-on-Tees, and one of those three original brothers who founded the company was my great-grandfather. If only I'd known, I could at least have heaved a shovelful of coal into great-grandfather's boiler.

Chapter 3

Bluebells and Beams

Strood was the halfway point on my trip around the south-east in terms of miles travelled. In a sense, it also represented a halfway point in the history of steam. I could cheat here, to keep a neat chronology, but that would make the journey so convoluted as not to be credible; so I shall continue on the page as I continued on the road.

I left Rochester and headed for the town of Tenterden. It is a place that shows every sign of comfortable prosperity, neat and certainly not gaudy. Crisp white weatherboarding alternates with another local building technique of hanging tiles on the wall. Tenterden has been described as the 'Jewel of the Weald', a name which has found much favour with the local tourist board. It certainly sounds more appealing than the original Tenet-ware-denn or Men of Thanet's Pig Pasture. It was a town which thrived on trade, notably in wool, and had the advantage of being a member of the Confederation of Cinque Ports, for it stood on the navigable River Rother. There are many reasons for visiting Tenterden, but the main attraction for me was that this Wealden town was once an important part of a railway empire. It was an empire unlike the huge groupings of the early railway age, one made up of a multitude of small lines from the very end of the railway construction period. One of those lines was the Kent and East Sussex Railway.

Although we are just setting off on our first railway journey, visiting a line not opened until 1900, there is a tenuous connection with the last trip. The man who had control over the line had previously been responsible for improving the navigation of the River Medway. He was Colonel Holman Fred Stephens, one of the railway world's many eccentric characters. His father was an art critic and pre-Raphaelite, and the Christian name Holman was in honour of Holman Hunt. But young Stephens showed little interest in anything except engineering, and an Act of Parliament of 1896 gave him the opportunity to rise in his chosen profession. That act authorised the constructon of light railways. Britain was well served by extensive main-line and branch-line networks, but there were gaps to be filled. There were industries looking for improved transport, small towns that wanted to be plugged into the system. Their needs were often modest; no necessity for fast expresses to thunder through. What was required was a scaled-down version of the main line: lighter rails to hold lighter trains moving at slower speeds and in no need of the panoply of regulations and safety precautions which applied to the main lines. The act allowed for such railways to be built and, importantly for railway promoters, did away with the need to apply for a separate Act of Parliament for each new line. So a network of little railways, some narrow gauge, some as here standard gauge, grew up inside the main framework. Many of them were to be controlled by Colonel Stephens from the headquarters of the Kent and East Sussex Railway, at the less than imposing address of 23 Salford Terrace, Tonbridge.

The hallmark of a Stephens railway was economy. Stations were built cheaply, rails were light, locomotives and rolling stock were bought new only as a last resort. As neither passengers nor freight alone could supply a profit, mixed trains were the order of the day. Passengers found their journeys interrupted while trucks were removed from or added to the train. Safety rules were relaxed, though some practices were rather beyond what Parliament intended. The practice of guards moving from carriage to carriage along the outside of the train caused a certain alarm among passengers. Similar tales could be told throughout Colonel Stephens' kingdom; and something of the atmosphere of those days still hovers around the Kent and East Sussex Railway, though not, I hasten to add, with regard to safety.

Tenterden Station may seem basic, and offer the minimum of facilities for passengers, but it was by far the grandest station on the line, and was a masterpiece of sturdy design in comparison with the corrugated-iron engine shed at Rolvenden. In that respect, the new owners have outdone their predecessors in building what is a rather grand new carriage and wagon workshop at Tenterden, using traditional materials and a design which fits in with

the station across the tracks. I am not sure that Colonel Stephens would have approved of such luxury. He would, however, delight in the new buffet, which started life as the offices of the Maidstone and District Bus Company – part of the country's first purpose-built bus station – and which the railway was actually paid to take away. It served as a buffet for a while, but had now become the Colonel Stephens museum. He would have approved of that as well, and would have felt at home with the mixed collection of locomotives and rolling stock.

Some railways pride themselves on preserving a particular image, of keeping true to the past of a line. If the line were, say, GWR, it would be run using GWR stock. The Kent and East Sussex is keeping faith with its past by using whatever is available that will do the job cheaply, efficiently and with a minimum of fuss. When you look at the pride and

The busy little saddle tank engine with its rake of vintage coaches epitomises the rural charm of the Kent & East Sussex Railway. (Donald Wilson)

joy of the line, the little 0-6-0* tank engine *Bodiam* which began service shortly after the railway opened in 1901, you might think that you have gone back as far as you can go. Not so; the engine was long in the tooth when Colonel Stephens bought it, for it was built in 1872 for the London, Brighton and South Coast Railway. It was one of a class known officially as A1X, but universally and affectionately referred to as 'Terriers'. There are two of these fine engines on the line, the second a youngster from 1876. The rest of the stock is made up of industrial and small tank engines, just the sort of thing that formed the backbone of every light railway. Among them come the USA and Hunslet Austerity class, built during the last war as workhorses with little in the way of refinements; in other words, good bargains. One of the American engines appeared with a mixed train of coaches to take us to view the Kentish Weald.

The British rail enthusiast, as a general rule, is a pretty insular sort of character, wedded to the belief that British engine design was not only the best, but the only proper design. Americans and other foreigners with different notions must, by definition, be wrong. There is no denying that as No. 30065 steamed into view it appeared to be a very un-British design indeed. The local style could be described as one of decorum, with working parts neatly tucked out of sight. The Americans let it all hang out. There is something of Heath Robinson about the odd collection of rods and cranks hung on the outside of the American train, which some find pleasing and others not. American practice means that parts are more accessible for oiling, maintenance and so on, but are more likely to suffer from occasional knocks.

---

* For those unfamiliar with this notation, it refers to the wheel arrangement. The first number shows the number of wheels supporting the front end of the locomotive, in this case none; the second, the number of driving wheels which move the engine over the track, in this case six, arranged obviously in three pairs; the third denotes the wheels supporting the rear end of the engine, again none.

I travelled in a coach which had been specially fitted out for disabled visitors, with access for wheelchairs and clamps to hold the chairs in place when aboard. It also has a special PA system which enables blind visitors to enjoy the trip and which can be used, as on this occasion, for general services. I chose the coach largely because it gave me the chance to chat to the guard during the journey. Not that he had that much time for conversation. This is a railway of comparatively modest resources which do not allow for the employment of crossing keepers, so the guard has to jump down to open and close the gates. This was less of a problem in the old days when the Light Railway Act allowed for ungated crossings, but reversed the normal priorities. Trains stopped to wait for cars, as they still do on a former light railway, then operated by British Rail, from Plymouth up the Tamar Valley to Gunnislake. A brand new diesel service was introduced, one which it was felt could dispense with the 'old-fashioned' sanders which give adhesion in the wet. The train duly stopped at its crossing, and was given clearance to carry on, but the combination of steep gradient and wet rails left the driver with furiously spinning wheels and no forward movement. The train was rescued and British Rail's latest wonder unit now carries a bucket of sand and a shovel. There are no such problems on the Kent and East Sussex Railway.

My intention on the journey out was to take useful notes on what I saw. In the event, I began by chatting to the guard and then discovered that a fellow passenger was a driver on the Ffestiniog Railway (see p.38). We talked about that as well and the trip was almost over before I began to pay any attention at all. The train stopped while the engine ran around to the front for the return journey, though we had not quite reached the end of the line. The last part of the five-mile journey was undertaken backwards and I looked out to what will be, for the

railway has plans for expansion. The aim is to extend the line to Bodiam, an opportunity to tap into a lucrative tourist market as Bodiam Castle is one of the country's major attractions. But they are a canny lot these light railway folk, and they are happy to wait until they have the funds from revenue to meet the costs of expansion. It will be a few years before the first train trundles into Bodiam Station, but they will get there.

Get there they did, and now passengers can enjoy steaming past the magnificent Bodiam Castle. There is now a new project to extend steam travel even further. The Rother Valley is planning to provide a steam railway link between the Kent & East Sussex at Bodiam and the main line at Robertsbridge.

On the return journey I turned my attention from railway chatter to the delights of the countryside. There are those for whom the train is all, and the only things that matter in the world outside are the severity of the gradients and the radii of the curves. For them, it makes little difference whether the lines are passing through town or country, past slag heap or cornfield. I do not share that view. From its inception, the railway has been a part of the whole life of the country, taking the businessman to his next appointment, the farmer to market, and the tourist to see the sights. It was the railway that first provided the means for ordinary men and women to get about and see things beyond the limits of home. Great travel firms like Thomas Cook had their origins in the railway excursion, and the train still provides as good a means as any to view the world.

To reach the railway I had driven from my home in Oxfordshire down the M25, where all your concentration is needed to cope with three lanes of speeding traffic, and along roads where the view for many miles was limited to the caravan in front, swaying like the buttocks of a ceremonial elephant. I had seen nothing. Now I had a window with a Vistavision view, steady progress at a modest speed of 15 mph and someone else to do the driving. For many, that is one of the great appeals of the train, but the cognoscenti add an appreciation of the subtle changes heard rather than seen, as the driver coaxes his engine along in response to changing conditions. It all comes together in a satisfying wholeness, for the train seems to become a part of the landscape, reflecting and responding to every change.

We are passing through ancient landscape here. Essentially all landscapes are ancient, but in some the present so heavily overlaps the past as to hide it from view. Here, the age is still in evidence as you steam through rural landscape of woods, fields and water meadows. Scattered across the land are the houses of the old yeomen farmers, and the oast-houses in which the famous hops of Kent were once dried but which have now largely been converted into 'desirable residences'. Woodland here means the forerunner of the dull, conifer plantations of the modern age: oak woods, planted at the command of Henry VIII to supply timber for His Majesty's Navy. Inevitably, there are new additions to the landscape, the most exotic of which is a crayfish farm, even if you do not actually get to see the beasts themselves.

The steam buffs wake up as the train nears Rolvenden and we pass sidings full of locomotives and carriages. They have a treat in store, thanks to a problem which has recently been plaguing the railway. Near Tenterden the railway embankment crosses a stream and the water has been weakening the whole bank. It has been necessary to install a new drain, and trains slow to little more than a crawl as they cross the workings. It so happens that this is at the point where the railway reaches its steepest section, a 1-in-50 climb. With no chance to take a run at the slope, the little engines have to earn their keep, and there is no sweeter sound to the enthusiast than the sharp, rasping blast up the chimney of an engine working hard.

The journey was over all too soon, but my visit was not yet over, for respects had to be paid to the man who engineered the line and ran it for so many years. Up the hill from the station, the local museum has a whole section devoted to the railway, and more particularly to Colonel Stephens. His desk and papers are there, the simple adjuncts of a working man's life, devoid of ostentation. Here, too, is a splendid collection of passes for railways around the world. It is interesting to note that though he and his assistant journeyed all around the British system, inspecting his light railways, they never travelled together in the same compartment. The Colonel followed the Victorian code that the master shall travel first class and the employee second. Such distinctions have disappeared from the Kent and East Sussex Railway, where everything is now first class.

In an ideal world, I should have continued my journey by rail, but the preserved railways owe their existence in good measure to the swinging axe of the late Dr Beeching, and as a result now exist mostly in isolation, divorced from the rest of the railway system. To travel from one to another, one has reluctantly to turn to the motor car. I drove on to Brighton where I was to spend the night, thinking how much nicer it would have been to have arrived in style at Brighton Station, a splendid confection in the Venetian style by the architect David Mocatta. Brighton is famous for its architecture, from the glorious absurdities of the Pavilion to the elegance of the Georgian terraces, and the station can stand comparison with the best. However, a consolation prize awaited me the next morning down the road at Hove.

A thick mist hung over the sea out of which the piers emerged like fantasy castles. Piers are fun, a little noisy and brash perhaps, but I have always enjoyed the combination of ornate ironwork, which can be as delicate as the Georgian balconies on the sea-front, and the robust solidity of the fairgrounds and amusements. Something of the same appeal carries over to the British Engineerium. Like Kew, it is a piece of solid Victorian respectability given visual confirmation in the building which, were you to remove the telltale chimney, might be mistaken for the local town hall. Again, like Kew, this was originally a pumping station built to supply the ever-growing demand for water in Brighton and Hove. However, it is not the reality of civic improvement that the visitor first sees inside, but an appetiser; though, like the antipasto of an Italian restaurant, it is an appetiser which leaves you almost sated, so packed is it with good things.

You enter at ground level and find yourself on the balcony of a great hall, a place of such grandeur that it takes considerable imagination to envisage its original role as a humble coal store. Now it is home to a vast collection of things steaming. There are full-size exhibits – a splendid traction engine and an even grander fire-engine of 1890 which is a mass of burnished copper and brass – and small-scale ones: models of stationary engines, paddle steamers, locomotives; in fact, everything we shall be coming across on our steam pilgrimage can be met here in miniature. I can look at such a collection only with awe for, given the finest tools in the world, the very best materials and a lifetime to complete the job, I would never match the workmanship of these creations.

I had a neighbour once who built model traction engines. I do not mean that he assembled prepared parts; he engineered everything from scratch. He once tried to assess the number of hours he had spent on a model, but as the total climbed into the thousands he gave up. To make such models can only be a labour of love, but then so is the business of bringing a Victorian engine back to life; only the scale is different. The small group who worked on the engines in Hove faced

some formidable tasks. The steam pistons of the pumping engines, for example, were seized solid, no easy task to cope with when the complete casting weighs up to two and a half tons. The results are there to see and yet, in a sense, remain invisible. The visitor can stand and stare at a gleaming, smoothly running engine and have no concept of the rusting, immobile hunk of metal it was not long before.

But before turning to the big engines, you have to tear yourself away from the exhibition hall, its models and its more frivolous Brighton attractions, which include a naughty penny-in-the-slot peepshow which today seems far less naughty than some daily papers. The approach to the engines is through a tunnel, down the middle of which runs a railed track, originally used for coal wagons. It leads, not surprisingly, to the boilers. There are four of them: Lancashire boilers of 1934, comparatively recent additions. A tiny turntable allowed the trucks to be sent into a coal store behind the boilers, and that store and the trucks are still in use today. Life is not so hard for boilermen these days, for only one of the four boilers is needed to keep the big engines ticking over for visitors. On reaching the machines you are faced with a choice: turn right to see the original engine of 1866, or left for the second engine, installed a decade later. That first engine, built by Easton and Amos, is a powerful beast, a compound with both high-pressure and low-pressure cylinders – the same system used on the *Kingswear Castle* to make the best use of steam pressure. Compounding makes for efficiency but it involves complications; and while this can be an engineering headache, it compounds the delight for the spectator. The already complex movement of rods and linkages in the beam engine become yet more intricate. The engine stands over a 160-foot-deep well from which it raised water, not just to ground level, but up to a reservoir which acted like a great cistern or header tank to send water at suitable pressure to all the users in the town. It originally pumped some 130,000 gallons an hour but that was not enough. The town grew and the Woolf Compound was added to provide a further 150,000 gallons an hour for the good burghers of Hove.

I went to watch the engineers starting up the Woolf engine. This is not a simple operation. These days most of us are used to starting machinery with a touch of a button or a turn of a key. Steam engines are not like that. Even if one ignores the fact that someone has to come in, light a fire, and start shovelling coal into the boiler long before the starting-up time, there remains a sense of excitement about getting the engine going. There is a holding of the breath, a 'will it, won't it?' question in the air. Dripping cylinder taps are the only signs of life from the engine, and the time has arrived for it to be coaxed into action. This is another huge beam engine and from one end of the beam a long arm runs down to a crank which turns a gigantic flywheel. Once this is rotating steadily, its momentum will ensure that all will run smoothly, and this is the first object of the exercise. Gears are engaged to set the wheel turning and steam is turned on. Then comes the critical point. The gears are disengaged and the engine is on its own. The arm sweeps round, the head of the crank edges to the top of its arc, and you can feel everyone willing it to tumble over the top to rush around for another cycle. It almost makes it, but then with a sigh it subsides and we are back where we started. Valves are checked. Is everything set in the right sequence? Another attempt, and this time the crank completes its revolution, the valves begin to do their work and vacuum pressure steadies down at 26 psi, the one sure sign that everything is in order.

This is yet another facet of the unique appeal of steam: the sense of uncertainty, the feeling of having to deal with a live thing which must be trained, coaxed and wheedled into behaving as you want it to behave. One could draw an analogy with a racehorse that skitters and bucks in the parade ring but, once the starting gates are opened, moves into smooth, powerful, co-ordinated motion. So the vast engine, when fairly set on its way, moves with a similar, effortless grace.

It seemed for a time that any rewriting of this section would have had to include a mournful paragraph on the sad demise of this wonderful site. Everything was up for sale, ready to be auctioned off, when a buyer, Mike Holland, stepped in and saved the day. If that had not happened the collection would have been dispersed to heaven knows where. At the time of writing, the whole site is undergoing a major refurbishment and should soon be reopening, and could be even grander than before. I shall certainly be along to find out.

There is certainly more to a love of steam than mere nostalgia, though when you turn back to the world of steam railways, nostalgia is obviously an important element in their success.

The Bluebell Railway, which runs from Sheffield Park to East Grinstead, plays the nostalgia card quite unashamedly. Everything is designed to persuade travellers that they are taking a journey into the past – not only into the age of steam, but further, to the time before British Rail emerged as a nationalised industry. It is, in a way, a somewhat curious notion because the great majority of the visitors to the line can have only a dim recollection of the period of independent railways which ended in January 1948. Yet the image does survive of a country carved up among a multitude of railway companies, each projecting its own personality. And there is truth in the image. The larger companies had their own engineering works, producing locomotives and rolling stock to their own design. They had their own working arrangements, their own style of building, and inspired devotion in their supporters. We live in an age when standardisation is seen as a good thing, which in economic terms it no doubt is, but perversely we yearn for diversity. Whatever criticisms might be levelled at the old railway system, no one ever accused it of a lack of variety. If that diversity had not existed, we should have had no need for so many preserved lines. One could stand for all, and I should not be writing this book. As it is, we can still revel in those differences that mark off one railway from another, that make a journey on the Bluebell so different from one on the Kent and East Sussex. So, to get the greatest pleasure, it helps to know something of a line's history.

Everyone in Victorian Britain, it seems, wanted to have a railway. For a railway was more than just a means of transportation: it put a place on the map. As a consequence, hosts of schemes were put forward, hundreds of lines proposed. Some remained confined to the pages of a prospectus; others managed to reach completion. Among these, if only just and with a little help from a friend, was the Lewes and East Grinstead Railway.

The story began in 1876 when locals decided to promote the line, but ambition outran support and they turned to their bigger brethren for help. The timing was propitious. Two companies, the South Eastern Railway and the London, Brighton and South Coast Railway (LB & SCR) were struggling for supremacy in the region. In all probability, neither was especially interested in the line, but neither wanted it to go to the opposition. In the end it was the LB & SCR who took over the running of the new line, which opened for business in 1882. It was a country railway serving a rural community, and that gave it its character. True, there were moments of high ambition for the little line, planned to main-line standards with double tracks, but realism prevailed and the second line was never destined to be used. It ran with modest

success until 1923 when the small railways of the area were gathered into one big group, the Southern Railway. Then along came nationalisation and stern looks at the railway system. Axes were sharpened and branches lopped, the old Lewes—East Grinstead route among them.

One day, someone looked back through the archives. The original Act of Parliament decreed that four trains a day must be run, and that obligation had been passed from the faltering Lewes and East Grinstead Railway to mighty BR. Thus the closure was illegal. This created a delay, long enough to allow local enthusiasts to put forward a plan for running the railway as a volunteer concern. And so the Bluebell Railway was born. It was a bold venture, for railway preservation was then in its infancy. The narrow-gauge Talyllyn was running, and the historic goods line, the Middleton Colliery Railway near Leeds, had been saved, but no one had yet tried to preserve a standard-gauge passenger line. In the summer of 1960, the Bluebell received its Light Railway Order and it has been running ever since.

It took me some time to overcome a reluctance to visit the Bluebell, a reluctance which could be laid at the door of northern prejudice. The name seemed to smack of southern whimsicality, not to mention Winnie the Pooh. The first preserved line in my native Yorkshire was a proper, serious line, a colliery railway which kept its real name. You wouldn't catch us calling a railway 'Bluebell' in Leeds. But the first visit won me over and subsequent visits have always been anticipated with enormous pleasure because, in the event, our northern colliery line and the Bluebell turn out to have the same appeal: the history shows through.

You notice it when you arrive at the main station, Sheffield Park, for at once you are faced with a question. Why on earth is that station here at all? Only history can provide the answer. There is no village, no town, but there is a large

Former London, Brighton & South Coast Railway 0-6-2 tank engine on the Bluebell Railway. (Bluebell Railway)

estate of the same name, whose gardens are opened to the public by the National Trust. It was this estate the station was originally built to serve. Why the estate should be so blessed is a question easily answered: Lord Sheffield was chairman of the Lewes and East Grinstead Railway.

The station has that comforting, homely atmosphere so often found on country lines. Main lines may seek to impress by the grandeur of their architecture, but the modest rural lines set out to reassure by their ordinariness, as if to convince the local rustics that no harm would come from these newfangled machines. The station could be a country house at the end of a sweeping drive but for the gaudy enamel advertisements which bedeck the walls and fences. 'Growing boys' we are told, 'need Virol', while Hudson's soap is declared to be 'powerful, easy and safe' – from which one might assume that other

soaps are weak, difficult and dangerous.

Travelling around the country's preserved railways, I get the feeling that they have acquired and put on display every enamel sign in the country. You can see why they are so popular. They instantly set a period feel: taking you back to the years between the two world wars, and providing instant nostalgia. Everything on the Bluebell line is designed to achieve this end. Take the signal box on the platform, for example. This is, essentially, a utilitarian feature which controls the movement of trains, and without which the line could not function. It has been decked out with all the trappings of the past – an oil lamp hangs in the window, a quill pen sits in the ink bottle. I do think this is going a bit far; even when the line was new they might have run to steel nibs. But I carp, for what really matters is that the re-creation of the features from the past which really count – the locomotives and rolling stock – is true to period. The Bluebell Railway has recaptured the individual flavour which the line had in the days before nationalisation spread uniformity throughout the region. This is by no means easily achieved.

The locomotives are predominantly south-eastern in origin, the early examples going back to the London, Brighton and South Coast Railway, later examples being dominated by the Southern. You can see a vast and impressive range of engines, from the Terriers, now well into their second century of work, right up to Bulleid's lightweight Pacific for the Southern Railway, *Blackmore Vale*. The Terrier, with its tall, copper-topped chimney and high bulbous dome, is the epitome of the small Victorian locomotive. The Bulleid Pacific represents a totally different way of thinking about design. Locomotive designers of Bulleid's time were conscious of problems such as wind resistance, so the engine was covered by a

smooth casing, disguising the lumps and bumps so prominent on early engines. Everything contrasts: the Terrier just over 26 feet long, *Blackmore Vale* at 67 feet. The old engine weighed in at a modest 28 tons, the Pacific engine and tender at 100 tons more. But what really counts is the tractive effort – the work that can be done. The more modern engine could summon up three times the power of the old, but was light enough for use on a modern branch line. Between these two extremes are all the variations which, in the years before nationalisation, gave a rural line its special appeal.

Locomotives are the glamorous end of preserved railways. The steam engine is the lure that brings in the crowds. You can, after all, find branch lines with attractive stations where the trains run through beautiful countryside and which are still in regular use by scheduled BR services. These trains are not packed out every weekend as the Bluebell trains are. But steam is only part of the mystique, for rolling stock does much to create the

The traditional signal box on the Bluebell Railway. (Peter Guest)

special atmosphere of the line. There are some 450 volunteers who give up their spare time to work on the line: drivers, firemen, guards, porters, signalmen, and the engineering staff. Others can be seen out on the line, the permanent way gang, and in the locomotive engineering shop, now among the few heavy engineering works left in Sussex. And some work in comparative anonymity on the carriages. The restoration of an old carriage is at least as painstaking a business as the restoration of an old locomotive. It can involve stripping right back to the frame; putting in new panels, new windows, new doors; painting, rubbing down, painting again, and repeating that process until the coachwork achieves that deep, rich gloss which is so immensely satisfying.

Out on the tracks on the day I visited was one quite magnificent coach – a London and North Western Railway observation car of 1913, a little off its old beat. This used to be part of a train running along the Welsh coast, its wide side windows and unusual end windows offering superb views of the countryside. It was, and is, a special coach and it looks as fine now as when it was first wheeled out on to the tracks. That is due to the efforts of the coach and wagon department, who sometimes ruefully refer to themselves as the Cinderellas of the railway. How much duller the scene would be without their efforts, which are not limited to the luxurious and the aged rolling stock. For many of us, to sit back in a seat in an old compartment carriage faced with fading sepia views of seaside piers and ornate hotels is to be taken back in time as effectively as by the distant blast of a steam whistle.

For the journey itself, one can relax and wallow in a particularly English idyll. The guard waves his flag and blows his whistle, the locomotive gives its answering blast and you move off into the sort of countryside the guide books inevitably call 'unspoiled'. For once they are right. It is still the countryside of the last century: of the small enclosed fields that took over from the open meadows of an earlier age; of hedgerow and fence and five-barred gate; of black and white cows munching among the buttercups, and farmhouses with walls hung with bright red tiles. There is the quiet wandering of the River Ouse, which provided the railway with one of its few challenges. It is crossed on a short viaduct and it is as well for the Bluebell that construction began before the age of the light railway. The viaduct was built to carry heavy trains, and big main-line locomotives can still use it. Woodland is a feature of the line: the old coppices of deciduous trees are surrounded in late spring by the flowers that give the line its name. This is not a countryside of dramatic highlights; it is, however, very much the countryside that exiles dream of; Browning's 'Home Thoughts From Abroad' in real life.

The line climbs, almost without interruption, from Sheffield Park to Horsted Keynes. The station at Horsted Keynes comes as a shock, for it is quite grand with its canopied platforms and subway connection. It can also boast a fine, well-preserved Victorian refreshment room on the central island, decked out in green and cream with a mahogany bar backed by mirrors. One would not be in the least surprised to find Trevor Howard briefly encountering Celia Johnson at a corner table beneath a stained glass window. Horsted Keynes, for the moment, is the end of the line, though plans are in hand for an extension to East Grinstead.

The Bluebell Line began because enthusiasts wanted to save the line and its memories. Today, like it or not, it has been absorbed into the leisure industry. The extension will double the length of the track but, more importantly, it will link it in to the British Rail network. That requires money and, even with a turnover for 1985 of over half a million pounds, extra capital is still needed. In 1986 a new share issue was floated and in the first three months £400,000 was raised. The issue was not intended for those seeking quick market killings and huge profits; it was aimed at people who wished to participate in an enterprise which had played an important role in the preservation movement. There are some who dismiss the whole idea as foolhardy, but I can only wish them well, as do the hundreds who turned up on a dull, drizzling day to ride the Bluebell.

In the event their optimism and faith was justified: the extension was completed and once again the Bluebell Line is joined to the main system at East Grinstead.

I made my way back to the car. If I had been reluctant to drive down the M25, I took even less pleasure in the journey back. The miseries of driving rain were intensified by the obliterating spray from speeding trucks. I would happily have exchanged that spray for a whiff of steam.

Chapter 4

Red Dragon

The Bluebell was among the first of the preserved steam railways, but it was not *the* first. It seemed appropriate to go right back to the beginning, and that meant a trip into Wales. So here, by way of an interlude before the next main theme, is a journey into the principality: the *Red Dragon* steam excursion. Even the most ardent devotee of preserved railways feels occasional yearnings to relive the delights of main-line travel, with express locomotives working as they were meant to work, hauling long trains full of passengers at high speed. The Bluebell Railway offers quiet delights, but you can hardly be said to be going flat out when the schedule allows you a quarter of an hour for a 5-mile journey. The *Red Dragon* was offering about 300 miles and speeds of 60 miles an hour, plus four locomotives working in pairs: the London Midland & Scottish Jubilee Class *Leander* with BR Standard Class 4 No. 75069 (the poor relation in the sense of being the only one without a name) for the outward journey; and a GWR double-heading of *Burton Agnes Hall* and *Drysllwyn Castle* for the return. It is the kind of event you anticipate for weeks, and it was a gloriously sunny day when I set out with a friend, Wayne Smith, who I suspect became a doctor only because no one would give him a Castle or a King to drive.

Didcot Station platform was crowded. There can be few more motley gatherings than those awaiting a steam special. There goes macho man, the Clint Eastwood of the public bar, beer mug slung low on his hip for a quick draw. There are the all-lads-together brigade in funny hats, staggering around with crates of booze. There is the serious practitioner with route map, stop-watch and notebook who will record meticulously every stop and start and change of pace along the way. There are the gricers, of whom more anon, swinging woolly hats and goggles and ready for action. There are even some quite ordinary-looking people, but they are outnumbered.

Experienced hands now waited for the traditional start to a steam excursion. It came just before the train was due: 'Passengers awaiting the 9.12 steam special are informed that this train is reported running twenty-one – two-one – minutes late.' No one looked in the least surprised. In the event we discovered that the train was ready at Ealing Broadway, apart from the minor disadvantage of having no driver. This problem overcome, we boarded with every expectation of the delays being compounded. Once you slip out of schedule you tend to lose your place in the train queue and move steadily backwards, but the delays proved to be the best thing that could have happened.

We travelled the first leg, from Didcot to Swindon, behind a diesel locomotive. Now the route is in itself both interesting and historic; it follows Brunel's original Great Western line down the Vale of the White Horse and ends at Brunel's premier railway town. But when you have come for steam, steam is what you want, and it is the thought of it that sets the nerve ends dancing. As we drew into the platform at Swindon, 700 pairs of eyes were centred on two objects: a long, powerful locomotive in BR black and, behind it, a second engine in the distinctive Midland livery of crimson lake. It was a coming together of two great railway traditions, not to say great rivalries. *Leander* was built at Crewe and the Standard 4 is a Swindon native, though, as GWR enthusiasts are always quick to point out, *Leander* was designed by Sir William Stanier, a man who learned his trade with the Great Western.

Uncoupling the diesel and coupling on the steam locomotives were accomplished with admirable speed. We set off merrily – and then stopped. The timetabling had caught up with us and we had to sit and wait while a service train cleared the track ahead of us. The wait was no great hardship and served to increase the sense of anticipation, for ahead lay a journey through superb countryside, full of interest. At last we got away and at the first junction swung off north-west towards Gloucester. This is where the enthusiast suffers divided loyalties between scenery and steam, although each calls on quite different senses. Obviously, you look at scenery while most of the interest in engines at work lies in the sound. You get occasional glimpses of the locomotives when the trains go round a tight curve, but you can hear the beat of living steam, and no two types of engine sound the same.

In this case the differences were marked, with *Leander's* three cylinders contrasting with the Standard's four. To the initiates the noise of the exhaust steam blasting up the chimney can play a theme as intricate as a Bach fugue. In our case, however, something had gone wrong with one of the players, for *Leander*, instead of issuing the appropriate sharp blast, was emitting a series of gasping puffs like an out-of-condition jogger. This was all too easy to interpret: steam which should have been working in the cylinders was blowing off, escaping uselessly into the surrounding air. It was no surprise at the end of the run to find the driver of the leading Standard full of praise for his locomotive's performance and scornful of that of his partner, which they had 'dragged along'. On the way up, I gave myself over to watching the world go by.

The first part of the journey is the so-called Golden Valley Line, and this is not an example of railway promoters'

hyperbole, but the actual name of a valley on the ordnance survey map, a leafy cleft through the edge of the Cotswold hills. The scenery throughout the first part was typical of the Cotswolds, whose special nature derives as much from the works of man as from the works of nature. This is limestone country, but the stone would scarcely be noticed if man had not quarried it and used it for his buildings. When freshly exposed it is quite pale, but left to weather it turns into a gloriously rich mixture of browns, yellows and umbers. You see it throughout the region in the walls of field boundaries, in houses and barns and in the stone slates of roofs, often turned even richer by the growth of moss and lichen.

Railway engineers try to avoid unnecessarily steep gradients, so a direct line from Swindon to Gloucester would have been difficult to say the least. The route, therefore, follows a northerly direction before swinging down the Golden Valley to Stroud, where it turns north again on the flatter lands of the Severn Valley. It offers something more than a trip through attractive countryside, dotted with lovely honey-coloured stone houses and small villages, tightly turned in on themselves. It offers a glimpse of an older industrial age. Railway engineers were not the first men to struggle with this intractable landscape, for canal engineers had faced the same problem a century earlier, when building a waterway to connect the Severn with the Thames. They too discovered that the geography dictated the route. So one finds canal and railway running side by side with one difference: the railway is still active but the canal is largely derelict. There are hopes, however, that the Thames and Severn Canal will be brought back to life, and at one stage I was asked to help accomplish it.

The Thames and Severn Canal Society had applied for a place in BBC Television's Sunday night appeal, and was given permission to make a short film showing the delights of the waterway and explaining what needed to be done. I agreed to present the programme, and over a sunny weekend we set about filming. A feature of the route is the long Sapperton tunnel, one end of which had already been restored so that its handsome classical portals gleamed in pristine splendour. The other end was a shambles, with work just beginning. There were only a couple of inches of water in the canal, so I walked down the middle in gumboots, praising the restoration work before disappearing into the darkness of the tunnel mouth. I have to confess I did not walk through – yes, we do cheat occasionally – instead we all packed up and drove to the far end. There I splashed back into the tunnel in order to emerge again from its darkness, chatting away to the cameras. 'Action' said the producer, so on I walked, straight into a large hole in the bottom of the canal where the water was more like two feet deep. I used, as they say, 'language' and I am told that the original tape is still circulating in the BBC. So whenever I see the Thames and Severn Canal, my first thought is not of its scenic splendour but of wellies full of water.

The railway crosses the canal very near the source of the Thames, runs over the top of the Sapperton tunnel and disappears into its own Sapperton tunnel to re-emerge in the Golden Valley. It is a narrow, beautiful vale and Cotswold stone is again everywhere, but the buildings are often larger than mere farms, for we have reached what was in its day an important industrial centre with the town of Stroud at its heart. All along the route you can see sheep grazing the fields and hills. At one time those fleeces were turned to wool and yarn. There were literally hundreds of mills along the rivers that radiate out from Stroud, taking their power from waterwheels and then, at a later date, from steam. Some remain, though few are now concerned with wool production. Those whose notion of a textile mill is Blake's description of

darkness and Satanism are astonished to find that these are handsome places; Georgian houses expanded in scale but with the same sense of proportion and the same local stone. I have spent many a day exploring these mills, so this was a way of seeing old friends from a new perspective.

Chalford's mills are among the most attractive and you can also see an odd circular tower, which is one of the few remaining lock cottages. It is a scene I delight in, and one which helps to explain why a railway company should go to so much trouble and expense to build a line through such difficult country. There was a thriving industry to be served.

The next section of the route is dominated by the Severn: up one side to Gloucester, past the cathedral and over the river in a flurry of bridges – our rail bridge, the new road bridge and, grandest and oldest of them all, Thomas Telford's stone bridge. The latter no longer fulfils any particular function but, for once, the authorities realised that it was too good to destroy.

Down the west bank, the line runs between the river and the Forest of Dean, which appears mostly as a distant fringe of woodland. The river is the dominating presence, possessing on that day an ethereal if not eerie beauty. It was oppressively hot and the air seemed scarcely able to contain its moisture, so a misty haze lay over the water. Soft, gently grading colours dissolved into one another so that there seemed no obvious distinction between sky and river, river and land. In this motionless calm we appeared as busy, noisy intruders, but we added our own pale strokes to this soft landscape with our drifting clouds of steam.

The Wye joins the Severn at Chepstow, and the bridge across the Wye takes you from England into Wales. The Wye is a more obviously picturesque river than the Severn – the viaduct is high and mighty, a castle looks down from the hill – but I ignored this temporarily to admire the driver's smooth, smart pick-up from the slow river crossing to speed on towards Newport. Sometimes one can have too many good things at once.

A little further down river, old bridges gave way to the new, and we passed under the elegant Severn Road Bridge. The Severn was a bit too wide and deep for the railmen, so their crossing is not only less spectacular but, to all intents and purposes, invisible. They went under the river, and all you can see is the sign announcing the Severn Tunnel Junction. There seems to be no end to the ingenuity in getting across rivers, but when you reach Newport you find the Usk crossed by one of the oddest structures of all: the transporter bridge. There was always a conflict between bridge builders and other river users: the road travellers find a low bridge convenient, but it gets in the way of ships. The transporter bridge was one answer. The basic structure is tall enough to allow big ships underneath, and from this a mobile platform is suspended. Drive or walk on to the platform and the whole thing carries you across – like a ferry which is suspended rather than floating. I did catch a glimpse of this interesting structure, but matters close at hand demanded attention.

It was railway weekend at Newport, and, as we pulled in, out went the 1933 LMS locomotive *Princess Elizabeth*, in her day a world beater. There was some cursing until it was realised that she was chugging out of the station then running back in to give short rides to visitors. It seemed absurd to see so much power given so little freedom. There was plenty of time to enjoy the sight of this exalted locomotive, for our engines had to go through complicated manoeuvring over a triangular network of rails to reverse them for the next stage. Then there was a further pause while they took on water. There was plenty of time to browse among the railway stalls set up on the platform, and to listen to the disco music provided by British Rail who must have

realised how bored we all were with listening to steam engines, and how we longed for teenage music blasted out at full, inescapable volume.

Thus it was with little regret, Elizabethan charms notwithstanding, that I waved goodbye to Newport for the last outward leg of the Usk valley route to Hereford. It ran along the edge of that series of high ridges and deep hollows known simply as The Valleys. This is border country in every sense: between England and Wales and between rural and industrial areas. Yet although it is close to the heartland of industrial Wales, the world of coal, iron and steel, it still retains an aspect of wild beauty. Even in the days when the valleys were a mass of

Former GWR locomotive *Drysllwyn Castle* simmering gently at Cardiff station, waiting to take over the rail excursion. (Anthony Burton)

smoking chimneys rather than straggling dole queues, there was still the world of the hills and the moorland to be enjoyed.

Soon the train moved on to the Welsh Marches, passing beneath the shadow of the Black Mountains through that much disputed land that divides the two countries. Hereford Cathedral provided a fittingly dramatic silhouette to mark the end of the run: the outward run, that is, for now there was the splendid prospect of turning around and doing it all over again.

Some find this notion rather unenticing, as though on that first run you could have seen and experienced all the journey had to offer. You could, in fact, take such a journey a dozen times and still come back with fresh enthusiasm, certain that there were discoveries yet to be made. Our age puts a special value on novelty and seems to have lost sight of the fact that places change, and that you the spectator change as well. The valley in summer is not the valley in winter, nor is the town you knew in youth the same as in later years. I have never minded travelling the same path twice. In any case, the return journey was to take on a very different aspect.

Our first locomotives were to go, their places being taken by a pair that shared a common ancestry in the Great Western Railway, *Burton Agnes Hall* and *Drysllwyn Castle.* They owed their being to one of the great engineers of the century, George Jackson Churchward. He introduced standardisation into the muddle of nineteenth-century railway design; brought in the tapered boiler, such a distinctive feature of GWR design; re-thought valve motions and boiler feed and even – rare indeed in a British engineer of that period – went to see what was being done in other countries. His work was continued and developed after his retirement and among the results were two outstanding classes of locomotives, the Halls and the larger Castles. We were to have one of each, and each was resplendent in GWR green with the hallmark of the company, the gleaming copper-topped chimney, on display.

Scenery-viewing time was now over, and the return journey was to be devoted to the time-honoured practice of gricing. I am not certain of the origin of this word or even of its spelling for I can find it in no dictionary, but I can recognise a gricer when I see one. He, or she, is to be found in a railway environment and can be recognised by a characteristic display of woolly hat and goggles. Seen in its natural habitat of the railway carriage, it will at once go into its routine of jamming woolly hat on head, goggles over eyes and sticking head out of carriage window at a point directly beneath a notice saying 'Passengers must not lean out of carriage windows'. There the true gricer will remain for as long as the train is in motion. The hat keeps cinders from the hair, the goggles protect the eyes, and the gricer's only aim in life is to breathe an atmosphere of hot smoke and listen to the beat of the engine. I joined my gricing doctor at the window and there we stayed for most of the return journey.

You do see the world when gricing, but concentration is centred on the driving force at the head of the train. It was a quite magnificent journey. The first pair of engines had been like out-of-step dancers but the Hall and the Castle achieved instant compatibility. There is no mistaking it; the beats of the two engines may not coincide but they can harmonise, and harmony was just what they achieved.

We departed almost an hour later, having strayed even further from our original schedule, but no one was unduly concerned as we made our progress through the countryside – a royal progress you might call it, for hundreds had turned out to photograph, record or just wave at our train. You can ride all day in a 125 and no one will take a blind bit of notice, but everyone loves a steam train. Children are called out of houses, motorists try to keep pace on adjoining roads and everyone looks happy and smiling. It seems that steam trains give almost as much pleasure to the spectators as they do to the passengers. Some people leave you in no doubt that they are there by design, not accident. One car sped along the road beside us, a Hall brass nameplate on its roof-rack to match the locomotive. It adds to the gricer's pleasure to know that 'his' train is spreading so much happiness.

However, we were to have a special treat that day. The long strenuous climb up Sapperton Bank lay ahead and we were still behind schedule. The drivers decided to give it their best. Regulators opened wide and the blast from the chimney took on a new, staccato urgency as we stormed up the slope. The effect was like the winning goal in the cup final. All down the train hands were raised in salute, fists shot up in recognition of the effort being made. We could see, in our mind's eye, the sweating firemen and the eager drivers and every gricer wished he was up there on the footplate. Among the ranks of the non-gricers, however, there were many who neither knew

nor cared about the efforts being made. One gentleman sat quietly reading, of all things, a Latin syntax. Rather larger numbers snoozed, some no doubt from tiredness, though the piled-up cans of McEwan's Export hinted at other causes. But we gricers had the best of it and at the end of the trip, when the engines were uncoupled and steamed away, we gathered to applaud them. How often do you hear clapping and cheering on a railway platform? The applause had been earned: the drivers had brought us back on schedule but, far more importantly, they had shown us steam at the height of its power. I did not know it at the time but it was a farewell appearance for the driver of the Castle, his last trip for British Rail, and for the occasion his old fireman from steam days had come back to join him on the footplate. What a farewell, and what a day for him to remember.

It had certainly been a memorable run with the *Red Dragon*, one of the best I have ever known. It had also whetted my appetite for further sampling of the hot, steamy breath of the dragon of Wales.

Chapter 5

Scenery and slate

Scenery and slate: the twin themes that dominate on the Great Little Trains of Wales – themes which have interplayed for the last hundred years, even if recently the former has been given more prominence. Today, we come to the lines built for slate haulage principally to enjoy steaming through mountainous regions. The Welsh railways offer a pleasing diversity, though there is a common theme suggested by that word 'little', for Wales is the birthplace of the narrow-gauge steam railway. There are many lines one can visit, including that interesting anomaly the Vale of Rheidol Railway, still run by British Rail, the last corner of that domain where steam still rules. However, I want to concentrate on just three lines, for each has unique qualities which complement one another to give a composite picture of the Welsh preserved railways.

I began my little train pilgrimage with the Talyllyn Railway, the line which will always have a special place in the affections of railway enthusiasts because it was here that the whole steam preservation movement began. In fact, there are many more reasons than that for visiting a line which, over the years, has become a great personal favourite. It has always had about it an air of slight eccentricity, beginning with its name. Tal-y-llyn exists all right, that is no problem, but the railway simply does not go there, never has gone there, nor was it intended that it ever should go there. It is easy enough to discover why the line was built. It served, as did so many small Welsh railways, to bring slate from quarries in the hills to the nearest port. These slate lines tended to be built by Welsh slate men. The Talyllyn was built by Manchester cotton men in

response to a war fought on the other side of the Atlantic. The American Civil War was a local affair with international implications, for the North blockaded the ports of the South and that dried up the supply of cotton to Lancashire. Mill owners, looking for new ways of investing their money, turned to slate.

The quarries at Bryn Eglwys were productive but access was difficult. The idea was mooted of a railway from the mines to what would be a new port at Tywyn – just the thing for Manchester businessmen keen to set their money to work. The original line climbed steadily for six and three-quarter miles up into the hills and was, from the first, intended to be worked by steam locomotives and to carry passengers. Above that point the route was a purely industrial line, worked partly by locomotives, partly by horses and by cable haulage up the steep inclines. The planning left something to be desired for passenger traffic. Only a small gap existed between the sides of bridge abutments and carriages. 'Too small for safety' declared the inspector, so what was to be done? No one was keen to rebuild every bridge along the line so a compromise was agreed. The track would be moved sideways in the bridge holes to give good clearance on one side, and virtually no clearance on the other. So, for safety's sake, the doors and windows on the narrow side were closed and permanently bolted. This was fine, unless there was an accident and the coaches toppled over closed side uppermost, in which case the unfortunate passengers were stuck until help arrived. The inspector, however, thought the risk acceptable. The Talyllyn began life with one-sided trains and has continued to run in this lopsided fashion ever since. It can quite literally be described as an eccentric railway.

This was only one of the oddities surrounding this little line. Passengers could hire trucks for the day in which they would be hauled to the summit, uphill all the way. They could picnic and stroll among the hills with no worries about missing the last train home, for what is uphill one way is, inevitably, downhill the other. Many a family outing, it is said, ended with everyone heading cheerily downhill, trusting in providence and the hand brake, not a practice encouraged by the modern railway inspectorate. More conventional travel was almost equally exciting. The first two locomotives delivered suffered from complementary defects: No. 1 *Talyllyn* bounced up and down, while No. 2 *Dolgoch* swayed from side to side, an intriguing combination if they ever ran double-headed. The problem of No. 1 was solved by adding a pair of trailing wheels, converting it from an 0-4-0 arrangement to 0-4-2 and this still runs happily today.

No. 2 was more difficult, as the odd motion was due to the length of the crank. You can do little about that short of redesigning the entire motion, and as there were no ill-effects it was left to continue weaving its way down the track. It too performs to this day. After this, later engines acquired from other lines seem disappointingly normal.

The story of the line in the twentieth century is one which is repeated throughout the country: the slate trade diminished and passengers were lured away by the new bus services. Dire events followed in quick succession. In 1946 work at the quarry was almost at a standstill, and then a mine collapse ended that story. The owner of mine and railway, Sir Henry Haydn Jones, maintained a passenger service, but when he died in 1950 his widow showed an understandable lack of enthusiasm for a few miles of rusting track, two Victorian locomotives in far from prime condition and a number of collapsing trucks and coaches.

Young admirers inspecting the footplate of Talyllyn locomotive no 4 at Tywyn. (Anthony Burton)

That might have been the end if author and engineer L.T.C. Rolt had not gone walking in the Welsh hills. He came upon the old line and fell in love with it. Meetings were called, funds raised, discussions held and the idea put forward that a group of volunteers might actually take over the running of a railway. The Talyllyn Railway Preservation Society was born and the railway preservation movement began. It is difficult today, with so many preserved lines, to understand how great an undertaking this was. Rolt called his account of the work *Railway Adventure* and adventure it most certainly was. We know how it turned out, but if you go to Tywyn raise your hat – or better still your glass – to Tom Rolt and the pioneers who made it happen.

One thing is certain, if the scheme had depended on the charm of Tywyn itself it would never have got started, for a drabber little seaside town it would be difficult to imagine. However, this means that even on the sunniest of summer days the railway is still more appealing than the beach. I am always content to settle down on the wooden seat of a one-sided carriage for a trip up into the hills.

Tywyn's Wharf Station was originally a goods yard where slate was unloaded either to be reloaded into larger wagons for the adjoining main line, or to be sent across the sea. Today it is a passenger station and museum, and a very good museum it is too. You can find out in advance about the journey you are to make or set off in blissful ignorance, try to make sense of what you see and check when you come back to see if you were right. I prefer the latter, the satisfaction of correct deductions outweighing the humiliation of the odd clanger. There is certainly no shortage of things to look at, for the valley we are to travel up has seen many changes.

The journey is a bit like Ravel's Bolero. It begins *pianissimo* and continues in a steady *crescendo* to end double *forte.* The line has a misleadingly quiet beginning, but the scenery becomes ever more splendid as the journey continues. We go through the outskirts of Tywyn to Pendre, where there may be more to look at, especially on a busy summer weekend, for these are the Society's loco sheds and there is a good chance of seeing coaling or watering of one of the engines. I rode up behind No. 3 *Sir Haydn,* an 0-4-2 saddle tank engine of 1878, built for the nearby Corris Railway and bought for the Talyllyn in 1951. It was fortunate that the Corris existed and that it closed just when the preservationists needed engines. The usual narrow gauge in Wales was a nominal 2 feet, in actuality 1 foot 11½ inches. The Talyllyn, somewhat perversely, was 2 feet 3 inches and so was the Corris. So no Corris, no locomotives to join No. 1 and No. 2 and, most probably, no Talyllyn today.

Early on, the members of the Society had to learn the virtue of adaptability. No. 6 *Douglas* is a delightful little engine with a very tall chimney, but just outside Pendre there is a very low bridge – an unhappy combination. There is the old joke 'don't raise the bridge, lower the water', which is pretty well what they did. They dipped the rails and you can still feel the switchback effect as you travel. At first, the route lies within the broad expanse of the river valley, a countryside of small fields of sheep and wet, marshy river edges occupied by flocks of water birds. The line heads straight through it all, and alongside and backwards and forwards across it goes the old road, the cart track from the quarries. So much seems to revolve around the slate workings, it is easy to forget that man was living and toiling here long before the miners came. There are memorial stones from the Dark Ages, Iron Age fortifications, and laid out in the valley is a pattern of farming unchanged for centuries. This is sheep farming with summer grazing on the hills and wintering in the valley.

The train steadily climbs away from the sea, and Rhydyronen Station marks a turning point as far as scenery is concerned. It was once quite an important stop on the line. There was a slate quarry here and a manganese mine nearby which provided a steady traffic, so a neat station building was provided, built, inevitably, of slate. At this point in the journey the enthusiast can not only feel and see the engine climb, but can hear its staccato rhythm as it labours upwards on a great sweeping curve, designed not to ease the gradient, but to satisfy local interests. The farmer who owned this land in the nineteenth century was sufficiently influential to insist on the detour. To the south, the hillside rises steeply above the line, which passes over a small stream. In Victorian days taking the waters was an infallible cure for practically anything but especially recommended for 'nervous exhaustion', a curious complaint which seemed to affect only the wealthy and bored; the poor had to make do with old-fashioned physical exhaustion. This Chalybeate Spring could be sampled on the payment of tuppence per cup. No medical records survive to report its efficacy.

Those of a nervous disposition may prefer to leave the train here, for the railway clings ever more precariously to its narrow ledge while offering grand views of Cader Idris: 'tempest torn' as Dylan Thomas described it, though no tempests tore while I was there. From now on, the route is marked by hills and woodland and a guarantee of something interesting to see wherever there is a break in the trees. Brynglas offers a scattered hamlet and the remains of an old woollen mill and, spectacularly, the river that crashes down between the trees at Dolgoch is crossed by a tall three-arched viaduct. There is a glimpse of bubbling, cascading water before the trees close in again, the train slides into a siding and re-emerges at Dolgoch Station, almost lost under a riot of rhododendron blooms in early summer. Another mile of travel brings us to the original

terminus of Abergynolwyn. At one time the line continued from here as a purely mineral route. Perhaps it was too much for the nervously exhausted passengers sipping Chalybeate water to travel such an exciting stretch of line: cliff-hugging, rock-piercing, narrowly winding up the steep hill. But for those who enjoy an exhilarating journey there is more to come, for the Society finally managed to bring their passenger trains all the way to Nant Gwernol. And that really is – as it always has been – the end of the road for locomotives on the Talyllyn.

Tallylyn No 3 at the top of the line at Nant Gwernol: originally the route was extended by a cable-worked incline. (Anthony Burton)

Nant Gwernol was not, however, the end of the transport system. A steep path rises up from the station and this too once carried rails along which empty tubs were hauled by cable, the first of a series of inclines carrying the line up to the slate workings. You can walk that old line, discover abandoned trucks and winding drums and all manner of bits and pieces left behind from the old days. I have described this route in another book, *Walking the Line,* but as this book is really about steam, not walking, we shall not travel far along the route. It is, however, a major part of the attraction of this line that it brings you to such scenery and then gives you time to walk and enjoy it at your leisure, providing you pay due heed to the timetable. Passengers can no longer, alas, hire their own trucks for a rollercoaster ride back to Tywyn.

The Talyllyn was the first preserved railway, but if you want to go back to the very beginning of the narrow-gauge story, you can do so. You can leave the train at Tywyn and drive north or, better still, you can take a train along the old Cambrian railway route. What a delight that is, with railway treats galore. You pass through Fairbourne, or you can stop there and enjoy a ride on the miniature Fairbourne Railway, which runs in and out of the sand dunes to the edge of Barmouth Bay. Carry on and you come across the main line which runs over one of the country's few surviving timber viaducts, then past the ruined splendours of Harlech Castle and exotic Portmeirion to Porthmadog and the Ffestiniog Railway.

The Ffestiniog started without steam locomotives and without its second 'f'. Welshification of the name is a recent event. The story begins at the start of the nineteenth century when the mouth of the Glaslyn was just a vast marsh. This was not, of itself, important but inland was Blaenau Ffestiniog, the capital of the Welsh slate industry, which had been prevented from achieving its full poten-tial by atrocious communications. The Member of Parliament for Boston in Lincolnshire, William Madocks, suggested building a sea wall, an embankment which would stretch across the estuary and behind which the marsh could be reclaimed. Quite how an MP for a constituency on the east coast of England became involved in a scheme for the west coast of Wales is unclear, but then several unlikely persons added their support, including the poet Shelley, a man associated more with skylarks than civil engineering projects.

The scheme went ahead and an embankment, The Cob, was completed in 1811. A new port was constructed, not perhaps as grand as its protagonists had hoped, but one that was to prove of considerable importance over many years. The English influence was acknowledged in the use of the name Boston Lodge for the settlement on one end of The Cob, and in the name of the new port that developed at the other end – Portmadoc. The latter has, like the railway, had its name subtly changed to Porthmadog, with the suggestion that it owes its origins to Prince Madog of Wales – a gentleman who, it is said, reached America before Columbus – rather than Mr Madocks of England. There is logic behind both claims, for Madocks the promoter and the seafaring prince, and no sane Englishman would dispute the origin with the locals. It is, however, beyond dispute that a quarter of a century after its completion The Cob was endowed with railway lines.

The line was built to carry slate from Blaenau Ffestiniog high in the mountains down to the shoreline and across The Cob to Porthmadog. The steam age was well under way, but no one seriously contemplated using the early engines on a line which, because the terrain is full of tight curves and steep inclines, had been built to the narrow gauge of two feet. This is not surprising when one considers that as late as 1825 it was still thought necessary to provide stationary engines to haul trains up the modest inclines of the Stockton and Darlington Railway. The Ffestiniog line, then, was to be a tramway where horses would haul light trains up the mountains, and gravity would do most of the work for the slate trains travelling down. At first, there were no passengers on the line, unless one counts the horses who travelled in style on the downhill run in special wagons called Dandy carts.

The engineer who built the railway was James Spooner, but it was his son, Charles Spooner, who first experimented with steam on the line in the 1860s. The job of building the first narrow-gauge locomotives went to a London company, George England of New Cross. The locomotives were successful in that they *did* work, but according to contemporary accounts they were somewhat alarming: 'A speed of eight or nine miles an hour is the greatest at which it is possible to run without incurring the risk of breaking the springs or loosening the driver's teeth.' The threat to footplate dentures was largely removed with the introduction of Robert Fairlie's double-ended locomotives. These were to prove remarkably successful and the design is still in use today, providing a unique feature for this line. They are quite extraordinary. At first glance they look like the results of a serious shunting accident: two engines which, having backed into each other, are irretrievably fused together. What you have, in fact, is two boiler units and engine units, each mounted on its own bogie, then joined together with the cab in the middle. The bogies enable the engines to cope with the tight curves and the double boilers ensure ample power for the hills. Remarkable they may be, but the Fairlies proved that narrow-gauge railways could work in even the unlikeliest of regions.

Over the years the little railway gradually changed its character and more conventional locomotives appeared in the engine sheds. Passengers began to arrive too. Shelley had recognised the romantic nature of the scenery, and tourist coaches were attached behind the slate wagons. So things continued and the line might have fared better but for grandiose dreams which led the Festiniog company to promote a second, even longer line, the Welsh Highland Railway, which was a dismal failure. The new line had little freight and fewer passengers, for with masterly timing it joined the transport scene just as the motor bus was beginning to thrive. Even the ubiquitous Colonel Stephens, who briefly took control, failed to make much impression. Decline set in after the Second World War and continued until the preservationists stepped in. The railway company had never been wound up, so shares could be purchased and restoration put in hand with a minimum of red tape. The Festiniog Railway Company still run the line as they have done for more than a century and a half, making this the oldest railway company at work in the world. The only difference is that the majority shareholder is now a charitable trust and, as with other preserved lines, the Ffestiniog relies largely on volunteer efforts to keep in business.

The bald statement that the new trust took over the line might suggest that all that was needed was a simple handover, after which trains could be kept running as they had in the past. It was not that simple. Antiquated rolling stock had to be brought back into reasonable condition, for passenger trains had ceased to run in 1939. Locomotives were aged, looked aged and – worse still – acted their age. Track was in even worse condition than rolling stock, though the basic civil engineering was sound. Three years' hard work got the railway open from Porthmadog as far as Tan-y-Bwlch, but a disastrous turn of events brought progress to a halt. The Electricity Board obtained a bill permitting them to flood land above Blaenau Ffestiniog to create a reservoir; land which included the little railway. The

railway opposed the plan, but the contest was uneven: the government-sponsored giant on the one hand and on the other a volunteer railway which was not even running trains over the disputed section. David was not going to beat Goliath, and the tracks vanished beneath the rising waters.

When you have started a battle to run a railway with a bank balance of nil pounds nil pence, you do not allow a little matter like submersion of the track to stop you. The railway fought for compensation and after a long battle, which was better news for the lawyers than the railway, some compensation was received. Work was begun on a deviation around the new reservoir to bring the line once again to Blaenau. In effect, a group of enthusiastic amateurs were setting out to build a railway. And they did: they surveyed a new line, built it and, in 1982, had the immense satisfaction of seeing trains running between Porthmadog and Blaenau Ffestiniog once again.

No one expects the tourists who crowd the railway to be concerned about the efforts involved in bringing steam travel back to these hills, but it is a heroic story, which should be kept in mind by passengers who marvel at a railway built in such unlikely surroundings. It is the sort of thing one might have found in a film from the old Ealing Studios, for it smacks of benign eccentricity. Who else but the British would volunteer to act as unpaid navvies to revive the fortunes of a railway begun a century and a half before? Who else would be content to work as their nineteenth-century predecessors had done, clearing the land with pick and shovel? Later, others helped, but at first it was down to the amateurs, and one is reminded of the original meaning of the word 'amateur' – one who loves. Many would regard the scheme as sheer madness, but what inspired madness it has turned out to be.

In a sense, starting at Porthmadog is doing the whole trip the wrong way round since this was the end of the slate run not its beginning, but we are looking at a tourist line not an industrial railway, and tourism has been a mainstay for a very long while. Even half a century ago it was being heavily promoted for sightseeing. 'The Toy Railway' the advertiser dubbed it in the Thirties, though this is not a term I would recommend using in the presence of any of those well-muscled amateur navvies.

Porthmadog itself is something of a tourist attraction, a place of rugged beauty almost surrounded by hills and mountains. On a fine day, apparently, you can see Snowdon. This, I must admit, is hearsay. I have often had pointed out to me the particular cloud under which Snowdon lurked, but the mountain itself has remained obstinately invisible. I have, however, walked by the harbour, filled with pleasure boats, and I have visited the museum to be reminded of the days when working boats dominated the scene. The old ketch *Garlandstone* has been preserved there. Porthmadog was also an important shipbuilding centre, creating craft for more than just the coastal trade of slate to England. Somewhat to my surprise, I recently came upon the brig *Fleetwing,* built here in 1874 and now lying abandoned by the jetty in, of all places, Port Stanley in the Falkland Islands. So there is more to Porthmadog than the slate trade and tourism.

A particularly important ingredient in the character of the place is its Welshness. The evening before I was to explore the railway, I scouted around the town for sustenance and found the Ship Inn. Outside was a board with a chalked menu. I made a valiant attempt to understand the Welsh but failed utterly, and might have moved on had I not eventually looked on the other side of the board where there was a translation for the benefit of visitors. There is a feeling that in Welsh-speaking North Wales the English are not always welcome visitors. This may be so, but no one could fault the Ship's hospitality or indeed its food, because it was far better than expected from a little pub in a small town. It put me in a good mood for the next day's travelling, and my expectations were not to be disappointed.

I woke to the sound of steam from across the harbour, pulled back my bedroom curtains and watched the locomotive prepare for the first morning run. This was *Mountaineer,* originally used for less peaceful activities than the tourist trade. It was one of many 2-6-2 narrow-gauge tank engines built to serve the trenches in the First World War. It has, like the railway's other locomotives, been converted to oil-firing. Throughout breakfast I heard the whistles accompanying shunting activity. This certainly increased the sense of anticipation, though it was less good for the digestion. Who wants to linger over food when the siren call is heard?

The station at Porthmadog is a utilitarian affair, plain but handsome, with no attempt to feed the taste for nostalgia. The Ffestiniog Railway is not trying to re-create past glories, but is simply part of a story that has been running for a century and a half. They are certainly not backward-looking in their procedures: quite the contrary. They had a computerised ticket system three years before British Rail, and efficiency is important for the railway is a major employer with forty-three permanent staff rising to over sixty in the summer season. And they need to be efficient, for there has been recession in the leisure industry too, with a falling-off in the numbers of passengers from a peak of 418,000 in 1974 to around 550,000 now. However, I can see no reason why the company should not prosper, for it has a great deal to offer.

I was to travel in some style in the first-class observation car, a luxury which for once is justified. Set at the end of the train, you get wide views on either side and behind, and on the return trip you get a close-up of the locomotive, thereby combining the best of all possible railway worlds. The nature of the line is established at once: hard work for engines, superb scenery and a twisting, convoluted route. You speed across The Cob, the embankment providing a perfect viewing point for the surrounding mountains, then the engine whisks through a right-angled turn to bring you to Boston Lodge, the site of the company's engineering works.

This was originally a quarry from which stone was taken to build The Cob, and the Lodge itself was home to the navvies. By the 1830s the repair works had been established and have been a centre for heavy engineering ever since. One or two bits and pieces have gone over the years. They once had their own small foundry, and you can see some of their handiwork in the cast-iron bridge at Crenan near Tan-y-Bwlch. Much remains, however, not so much because of its continuing value one suspects, but because of its sheer immovability. There are machine tools here a hundred and more years old, bedded on to great blocks of slate, so big that no one knows how far below floor level they rest. Here they not only do the regular maintenance work on locomotives – when I called in the double Fairlie *Merddin Emrys* was stripped down to the boiler and looked even odder than a Fairlie normally does when out on the track – but they take on major jobs, from manufacturing axles to rebuilding coaches. They have to do a lot of their own basic manufacturing here, because so much is unique. You cannot just ring up for an off-the-peg spare part for a Fairlie. This is a real engineering works which also provides training for locals. Unusually for this type of work, it is not a male monopoly.

Minffordd, the next stop, seems at first glance to be little more than a pleasant country station with a stationmaster's house, the latter, like others on the line, rented out to Ffestiniog staff. In its day, however, this was an important junction

where main-line standard gauge met narrow gauge, and a complex system eased the trans-shipment of goods between the two lines. Both lines still run, but now only passengers are exchanged, as the little line crosses over its larger neighbour. Minffordd is also a place of homage for many steam enthusiasts for the grave of Bill Hoole is to be found in its cemetery. His exploits on the expresses of the old London and North Eastern Railway (LNER) delighted the connoisseurs among his passengers, and some of his high-speed runs now belong as much to legend as to fact. It was said that officials and repair yards were less enthusiastic. Retirement from King's Cross brought him to Wales and Ffestiniog, and here he spent the last years of his life on the regulator. We shall not see main-line runs like his again.

After Minffordd the line remains for a while in a semi-urban environment, but one in keeping with the character of the railway, for wherever you look slate rules: slate walls divide property, slate roofs cover the living and slate headstones the dead. At Penrhyn the nature of the line begins to change as you cross a ridge to leave the bay of Traeth Mawr for neighbouring Traeth Bach, into which the Dwyryd flows, forcing its way between craggy hills. The railway itself is forced into an increasingly cramped space, clinging to the hillside. The river valley is glimpsed less and less frequently as woodland closes around, and one can concentrate on the problems faced and solved by railway builders in this inhospitable environment. Cei Mawr, the great quay, is a massive embankment over 60 feet high, built of drystone walling, and that is followed immediately by a cutting through the rock. The pattern of the line is becoming established. The aim was to climb from Porthmadog to Blaenau Ffestiniog, 710 feet, but this was not to be a steady ascent; there were hills and crags to wiggle around, valleys to circumvent, and the modern line had

This photograph of the Ffestiniog railway clearly shows the amount of engineering work involved in taking a line up such a mountainous route. (Ffestiniog and Welsh Highland Railways)

newer obstacles to overcome. An energetic crow would have a mere 9 miles to fly; the railway locomotive must go half as far again – 13 miles 54 chains, the company announces with blissful disregard for metrication and all its works.

You leave the valley of the Dwyryd as the train swings around the extraordinary tight bend known as Tyler's Curve, not for the revolutionary leader but a Board of Trade inspector. Now the line has to make a great U-turn. You can see the track on the hillside about a third of a mile away, but you have to travel over a mile and a half to get there, and when you reach the station the locomotive takes a well-earned pause for refreshment. It has climbed 430 feet since leaving Porthmadog, 7 miles away. This is Welsh hill scenery at its best

and many passengers stop off here to walk along the nature trail as I have done, not so much to inspect the rare plants as to admire the superb workmanship of the great railway embankment, and to walk up into the hills for an airy view of hardworking trains.

Beyond Tan-y-Bwlch, the railway enters truly wild countryside under the shadow of the rocky hill Moelwyn Bach to reach Campbell's Platform. As so often along this line, the name has a story. You can see the platform, a piece of level ground, and you can also see close by a solid stone house, which has the air of rugged self-reliance one would expect from a dwelling in such a lonely location. The stones have that rich patina of age which comes with exposure to mountain air for four centuries. The house was bought by Colonel Campbell who modernised it but did not, for a long time, have any road access created. This was not a problem with the railway so close at hand; each day he commuted to Tan-y-Bwlch on his own locomotive. It seems almost unreasonable that anyone blessed with such a house in such a situation should possess his own locomotive – to them that have … Mind you, I should be almost as happy with one of the little cottages built for railway workers where the trains hammer past the doors.

Up ahead lies the Tan-y-Grisiau reservoir which posed such a monumental problem. It swallowed up the line, which was bad enough. You can see that old line heading down to the water from Dduallt Station, and you can see how a new line would have to climb steeply to rise above the level of the water. How was this to be achieved? The answer was deviation. The line curves around sharply, climbing all the while to cross over itself on a wide spiral, gaining altitude and finishing up pointing back in the direction it started. On a busy day you can see the unusual spectacle of two trains on the same railway, one passing over the other.

This spectacular section completed, it was comparatively simple to carry the line down into Blaenau Ffestiniog. It is a dramatic approach; there are natural wonders such as the waterfall tumbling noisily down a cliff beside the tracks. More impressive, however, are the works of man, the mountains of shattered rock that ring the capital of slate. Some find it oppressive, and it is undeniably a monochrome scene of dull grey, seen at its best after rain when the slate fragments gleam and sparkle. No one could call it pretty, but goodness it overwhelms you. You need no interest in industrial history, no appreciation of the work of slate miners and quarrymen to enjoy the ride on the Ffestiniog. A majority of the passengers ask for nothing more than to enjoy a ride on a little railway in a very grand setting, but it is here at the end of the line that it all makes sense. How many thousands of tons of slate were sent down the line to Porthmadog? How many thousands more were broken and discarded to make spoil heaps the size of mountains? I find it a place of wonderment and anyone who shares my excitement at the first view of Blaenau Ffestiniog can do no better than visit the museums based on the old workings: the mines of Gloddfa Ganol and Llechwedd, burrowing deep into the mountains.

The success of the Ffestiniog Railway encouraged more narrow gauge construction to join local slate mines and quarries to Porthmadog to Dinas Junction, where it would join the main line of the former London & North Western Railway through Caernarfon. To describe progress as slow hardly does credit to the snail's pace at which things progressed. Work began in 1877 and the first part of the line was completed as far as Rhyd Ddu at the foot of Snowdon, with a branch to quarries at Bryngwyn. In 1905 a new company, the Portmadoc, Beddgelert and South Snowdon Railway, was formed to link to the Corris railway and provide access to more extensive slate workings.

There was still a gap in the middle, and that was filled when the Welsh Highland Railway was given a Light Railway Order to complete the line. It should have been a day of triumph when the lines finally opened throughout, linking Caernarfon and Porthmadog in 1923, but just four years later the company was in receivership. It was leased to the Ffestiniog and staggered on in service until 1937 when traffic ceased. And that should have been the end of the story. The line never received the goods traffic that it needed for survival. It was a difficult line to work, having been built on the cheap, but it passed through some of the most beautiful and wildest scenery in Wales. It was a perfect candidate for revival as a line that would tap into the success of the other little trains of Wales. In 2011, the Welsh Highland Railway was again open for business, not carrying slate and mineral ore, but tourists and, of course, rail enthusiasts, who were to be given a very special treat.

My journey started at Caernarfon. The station may have a romantic setting, standing in the shadow of the castle, but there is no romance about the buildings: a portacabin booking hall and a platform with a basic shelter. But who worries about things like that when you have a footplate pass for a ride on one of the most powerful class of narrow gauge locomotives ever built, an articulated Beyer Garratt. This is one of those locomotives over which enthusiasts positively drool, simply because it is unique. For those who don't know the engines, a brief explanation is necessary.

The story begins with Herbert William Garratt, a railway engineer in New South Wales, who was aware of the difficulties in getting enough power to cope with winding tracks in hilly countries – precisely the problem faced by the Ffestiniog that had led to the Fairlie design. Garratt's solution was even more radical. His locomotive would consist of three sections: at the front, a large

On the footplate of a Garratt locomotive on the Welsh Highland Railway: the driver is reversing onto his train at the start of the journey from Caernarfon. (Anthony Burton)

water tank, on its own set of wheels, with its own steam cylinders; at the back, the bunker, again with its own wheels and power unit; and in the middle, a large boiler and the cab. The front and back units could move independently of the central section. This meant that the locomotive could work round sharp bends, but also had a lot of power to work steep inclines. The locomotives were manufactured by Beyer, Peacock in Manchester and were soon being sent around the world. The locomotive on which I was about to travel was built in 1958 and once in the cab it was very obvious where it had started its working life: all the labels on gauges were in two languages – English and Afrikaans. This was a locomotive that had started its working life in South Africa and, as became increasingly clear as we got under way, was absolutely perfect for the Welsh Highland Railway.

The description that follows has to be in two parts for a very good reason: on the way out I was so engrossed by the working of the locomotive on this particular track that I never got round to making any notes about the scenery through which we passed. That had to wait for the return journey, when I sat in comfort in a carriage.

The journey began modestly, with a certain amount of to-ing and fro-ing to get the train on the running line, which involved the fireman hopping in and out to change points. One of the beauties of the engine is that it steamed so well, so at least he wasn't having to get on and off to add more coal to the fire at the same time. Dealing with a massive engine such as this might seem hard work to some, but the crew were unpaid volunteers, like almost all the footplate crews on the line. Then we were off, with a reasonably straightforward start on what was originally the old standard gauge main line, relaid with narrow gauge track. It is only when you reach the former Dinas Junction that the nature of the line begins to assert itself. The old main line went straight on, but the Welsh Highland at once swings through a great U-turn, and from the cab you have the odd experience of seeing the three parts of your locomotive pointing in different directions, but apart from the squeal of wheels on rails, the tight curve presents no problems.

Now we were going to start a long, continuous climb to a summit 648ft above sea level. The engineers who constructed the line were looking to save money by following the natural contours of the land, avoiding the expense of cuttings and embankments as far as possible. So this is very far from being a straight climb and now the Garratt really comes into

its own, swinging round the bends and, it seems, conquering the gradient with far less effort than you might expect. On a conventional locomotive, the fireman would be working almost continuously to keep up the steam pressure, and though he certainly wasn't idle he had a steady rather than frantic effort to put in. Once over the summit, there was an even steeper and longer descent with an average grade of 1 in 40 and ever-more extravagant curves. A series of short tunnels plunged the cab into darkness, apart from an orange glow from the gap in the firebox doors. If the fireman was kept busy on the ascent, it was the driver who had to concentrate hard on the downhill section. This is a heavy locomotive with a long train behind it: you don't want it running away with you.

Dramatic scenery on the Welsh Highland Railway: the Hunslet tank engine *Prince* started its working life on this line in 1906. (Ffestiniog and Welsh Highland Railways)

There are also problems seldom met on railways these days – several unmanned crossings, where the train slows and each side of the engine has to be checked, and even one where barriers have to be operated by the train crew. The final few miles to Porthmadog are a complete contrast to the rest of the line – straight and flat. Some two and a half hours after I stepped onto the footplate at Caernarfon, I said my goodbyes and thanks to the crew at Porthmadog station.

The station proved the ideal spot to wait for the return journey – no need to explore further: the sun was shining over the sea, the bar had real ale – and who could resist trying the splendidly named Bog Standard Bitter – and locomotives from both the Welsh Highland and Ffestiniog lines puffed by at regular intervals. There couldn't have been a better spot to have lunch. It was with a feeling of immense well being that I took my seat for the trip back to Caernarfon.

The start is unusual, as the train has to cross the Britannia road bridge, the lines running across the roadway on a diagonal, so the cars have to wait while the train rumbles over. Out on the mudflats, an array of wading birds were pottering about, beaks down, hoping for goodies. Then we crossed the Cambrian Coast main line and the next part of the journey is over very flat land. What is not at all obvious is that this was, at one time, all covered with seawater. This was the tidal estuary that was closed off when the Cob was built. Now it is all grassland, grazed by sheep. This journey took place in early April, so the spring lambs were to be seen everywhere. The ewes that had long since become used to their steamy neighbour chewed on steadily, but the young ones leaped and ran as fast as they could away from the strange monster. It is odd to think that the line of low hills out to the left were originally sea cliffs.

The line passes over the river once again, just beyond the Pont Croesor Halt. Close by is a protected site, where ospreys nest. I was told that sometimes they can be seen flying overhead or fishing in the river, but sadly there was no sight of these magnificent birds. At least the scenery was there to be enjoyed, the trackside ablaze with gorse and a backdrop of hills almost lost in a blue haze. A large, grassy hump close to the line was once an island lapped by the sea. Soon the track was leaving this reclaimed land and heading out towards the hills, one of which is an almost perfect cone, earning it the rather fanciful title, of 'the Matterhorn of Wales'. Its actual name is 'Cnicht', said to derive from the English 'knight' as it's supposed to look like a jousting helmet. To my eye it looks like a shapely hill, but has precious little resemblance to either the famous Alpine peak or an item of medieval armour. But the journey was about to become a great deal more exciting and the scenery far more dramatic.

The hills begin to close in on the line, which enters woodland, where trees emerge from a boulder-strewn landscape. Now we began the twists and turns that are such a feature of this line. A writer in the early nineteenth century described the Cromford & High Peak Railway as 'that corkscrew line': he clearly hadn't seen the Welsh Highland. Compared to this, the Derbyshire route is ruler straight. One big advantage of the line, as far as passengers are concerned, is that the bends are so extravagant, that if you manage to get a place in the open coach near the back of the train, you get excellent clear views of the engine at the front: ideal for photography. As we got deeper into the woods, the landscape seemed just the sort that would have inspired the Grimm brothers' more macabre tales: trees for which the word 'gnarled' could have been invented, surrounded by moss-covered stones that seemed alarmingly likely to topple down the slope. At times, the track briefly disappears into a deep cutting carved from the rock, before emerging to more woodland, with just the glimpse of an occasional house in a clearing. Then, quite suddenly, we emerged into an almost suburban cluster of houses, with neat lawns and flowering shrubs.

The route was heading for a gap in the hills, the Pass of Abrglaslyn, voted by National Trust members as the most beautiful spot in Britain, not that we had much of a chance to admire it at first. There was a brief glimpse of a little picnic area before we disappeared into a tunnel. Emerging in a cloud of smoke and steam, the line ran in the shadow of a high wall built up of massive boulders. This must all have been incredibly hard work for the men who blasted their way through this rocky terrain: there's a stone arch and almost immediately we are back into another short tunnel. The line is cut into the hillside and down below is the Afon Glaslyn, with a pathway of stones alongside, known as the Fisherman's Path. You finally get to see what the National Trust members were talking about, for this really is a spot to delight, with its crags and bustling river.

Once through the Pass, the scenery begins to open out, as the route follows the twists and turns of the river. There was a splendid panorama of hills coming into view, dominated by the looming hulk of Snowdon. There was a short plunge through Goat tunnel before the train arrived at Beddgelert. As we waited at a station, I looked out of the window to find a chaffinch looking back at me from his perch on a branch. I wonder what birds make of trains. Off again, the track goes into convolutions, passing through a miniature rock canyon, followed by the most extravagant curve yet as the line goes though a horseshoe bend and we were back with another meander through the woods. If one didn't know the route was planned to follow the natural contours, you'd assume the surveyor was roaring drunk when he drew up his plans.

Emerging from the woods we reached the summit and a really open vista of the attractive hills, not the dramatic craggy hillside of the Pass, but grassy and gently rolling: perfect walking country. A small lake came into view, and there is always something romantic about water in such scenery: the hills rising steeply from the edge, reflected in the still waters. There was hardly time to enjoy it before we were

One of the many advantages of travelling on the Welsh Highland is that, thanks to the many sharp curves, passengers have a chance to photograph the locomotive in action. (Anthony Burton)

once again off through a series of sharp bends. There is also a reminder of why this line was built, with tips from old slate workings. The much larger lake of Llyn Cwellyn, with its background of crags, has a halt by its side, the Snowdon Ranger Halt. It does, in fact, mark the start of one of the popular routes to the Snowdon summit, the Ranger Path.

The scenery changed yet again, as we steadily descended towards the coast. The fields are lusher and greener, and long lines of stone walls march up the hillsides from the valley bottom. We ran alongside the little river that emerges from the end of the lake. It rushes along and manages to take an even more convoluted route than the tracks. There are glimpses along the way, but when we finally emerged alongside it again, we were far above it. The final stage of the journey is through an altogether gentler landscape of farms and fields. The train coasted along comfortably, the sound of the locomotive reduced to a whisper of steam and the clatter of wheels. The high drama of the hills may have ended, but this is still attractive countryside, with hedges now taking over from stone walls and flowery meadows instead of rough pasture. The arrival at the line's depot, with its sheds, workaday diesels and locomotives waiting for restoration, meant the journey was nearly over. The line crossed the river for the last time and there was one final moment to enjoy, as Caernarfon's splendid castle came into view.

There are lines in Britain that offer all kinds of scenery along the way, some gently pastoral, others rocky and mountainous, but I cannot think of any that has quite such an amazing mixture as this line. It has been an absolute joy to travel, not to mention the wonderful opportunity of travelling on a fine example of a famous class of locomotive. There is, of course, one other very dramatic railway in this part of the world and one that offers a very different experience, the Snowdon Mountain Railway.

Much as I enjoy the Snowdon Mountain Railway, I always approach it with feelings of guilt. From my schooldays, I have been an enthusiastic climber and hill walker and it still seems wrong somehow to get to the top of a mountain and find that the only thing puffing from the effort is a locomotive. There seems to be an odd morality here that says I am supposed to earn treats like the view from the summit and not have them handed to me by someone else.

The Snowdon Mountain Railway is unique in being a genuine mountain railway; in being a private steam line run without volunteers; and in having broken with railway tradition by being based on a metric gauge long before the initials EEC had been heard in the land. The company, Snowdon Mountain Tramroad and Hotels Company, was formed in 1894. Given the usual methods of railway construction in the nineteenth century, it is astonishing to find that only 150 men were engaged in building the line from Llanberis to the 3,495-foot summit. The track, 4½ miles long, climbs for 3,140 feet, yet it took this modest workforce only four years to complete.

The engineers turned to Switzerland for the technology and opted for the Abt system; this employs two racks centred between the rails which engage with cogs or pinions beneath the locomotive. As a safety measure, the two racks are set out of phase. The gauge is 80 centimetres. Although the Swiss were the major users of the rack and pinion system on their mountain lines, they were not the first to adopt it. Two Leeds men, Blenkinsop and Murray, installed a rack system at Middleton Colliery in 1813. It was not merely the first rack railway, it was the first commercial railway of any kind. It has the further distinction of beginning the standard-gauge steam revival, though in more conventional form, and it still runs today. Blenkinsop and Murray were not, as some have alleged, silly men who thought smooth wheels would never grip smooth rails, but men who saw that heavy locomotives broke light track, and so overcame the problem. Their success was overtaken by the arrival of stronger rails, so in the 1890s it was to Switzerland that the Snowdon Mountain Railway turned, both for expertise and for locomotives. This caused some problems for the local engineers and led to some odd local names for locomotive parts. Why, for example, is the air valve called 'the loft'? Not because it looks like a home for pigeons or the top of a house, but because the original drawing was labelled in German '*luftvenlil*'.

If the original staff could come back to the railway, they would find little change since the first train ran in April 1896, except that they would be most unlikely to reach the summit so early in the year. The first four locomotives, delivered in 1895 and 1896, are still there and still working and the three newcomers from the 1920s are not substantially different. They are odd-looking affairs with sloping boilers, specially designed so that when they reach the most severe gradients the water remains level and does not uncover the firebox. You might wonder how this would work if the engine turned round, to which the answer is, it never does turn round because the method of working is also unusual. For the ascent, the locomotive is set behind the train to push, but it is not coupled. Apart from pushing instead of pulling, it works normally. Coming down is very strange. The locomotive remains in forward gear while running backwards and is, in effect, acting as a brake. It puffs out air instead of steam from the pistons, which are working as air compressors, offering interesting problems of lubrication and cooling.

'Summer' on the railways means any time from spring onwards, because that is when the new timetables come into operation; but not here. I arrived in April and was less fortunate than the passengers of ninety years ago; the upper part of the line was still blocked by snow. I was not too disappointed – it was not

Locomotive *Enid* and a vintage coach above the cliffs of Clogwyn on the Snowdon Mountain Railway. (Snowdon Mountain Railway)

my first visit and there was something adventurous about chugging up to the snow line, though a sense of adventure is not something the railway is keen to encourage. They are frequently asked for a single ticket so that visitors can ride to the summit and walk down. The company invariably refuses: not because they want the cash, though I dare say they do, but because of safety. Too many people regard a walk on Snowdon as a jolly country stroll and come ill-prepared for the mountain. The weather can change incredibly quickly even in summer, and in winter the narrow rock ridges can be caked with an almost invisible layer of ice. These dangers were brought home during my visit when a walker slipped off the rock and fell uncontrollably down the steep snow slope.

In such circumstances, the railway is often the first point of contact with the survivors of an accident, so officials are aware of the risks of the mountain. They cannot stop the ill-equipped and the ill-clad from walking, but they will not encourage them by selling single tickets. They would accept that this is not the cheapest rail ticket in the country, but this is not the cheapest railway to run. There are thirty-three permanent staff and over twice that number in the high season; the rack system suffers such heavy wear that replacement is like painting the Forth Bridge. The ticket is a lot cheaper now than when it first appeared. The return fare was 5 shillings, and drivers were paid 2 shillings and 5 pence a day. You can work out for yourself what the price would be given today's wages. Some of the railway staff have an unusual lifestyle. The summit station is permanently manned and offers an ideal post for the true mountain lover, like manager Ian MacGillivray who used to go up there in May and not be seen at the bottom again until October.

It was soon time to set off on the journey. I sat at the front with the guard, whose duties are again far from conventional. His main task is to sit staring concentratedly at the rack in front of him. He watches for obvious obstructions such as lambs straying on to the line, but more importantly he looks for the little things, a small rock or even a stone caught in the track which could cause a derailment. It is a comfort to know he is there, because once you get under way the track rises as steeply as a steam-powered rollercoaster. There is a straggle of houses, then it is off to the hills, and how very quickly the mountain scenery takes over, with a roaring cascade under a steeply-angled viaduct, quite an intriguing problem for engineers and builders. There are wider vistas which include slate quarries, inevitably, and those around Llanberis are, if anything, more dramatic than those of Blaenau Ffestiniog. Beneath the great terraces that lower over Llyn Padarn is the National Slate Museum and alongside is the narrow-gauge Lake Railway. But attention turns to the wider prospects of the mountains of Snowdonia.

To the north are the peaks of the Glyders and distant Tryfan; to the south, the ominous dark cliffs of Clogwyn D'ur Arddu on which are to be found some of the country's most difficult and strenuous climbs. There were no climbers out that day but plenty of walkers, some properly equipped, some absurdly clad in light clothes and green wellies. I would love to have stopped the latter and shown them the statistics of accidents caused by people wearing the wrong shoes in the wrong circumstances. Green wellies on icy rocks above thousand-foot drops are footwear as ill-matched with circumstances as you

The little train is scarcely more than a dot on the horizon as it climbs towards the top of Snowdon. (Snowdon Mountain Railway).

can get. I have been on mountain rescues, and carrying corpses down from the hills is a sobering experience. The only man that day who appeared to know what he was doing was in training for the Snowdon marathon, and he overtook us with apparent ease.

Small halts come and go: Hebron, named after a nonconformist chapel; Halfway, named for more obvious reasons; each manned, another job for those who like mountain solitude. We passed through the hill pastures where lambs cowered behind stone walls, looking as if they felt a bit premature entering the world, for recent snow still clung to the hills and a cold wind whipped up the valley. The views became wider and the snowline got nearer and nearer until we came to a halt at Rockey Valley, just over 500 feet below the summit. No one minded much because they had the chance to walk out into the snow and see some of the country's finest scenery in the crisp, clear air. I did regret a little that we were denied that final run up the rocky ridge and the view down the spine of Crib Goch, but the view and the day were great compensation.

When we set off on the descent, I mused over the problems of building this line. The men had worked right through the hard winter and my walk in the open air had shown me just how cold it could be, even in April. It was, in fact, just ninety years ago that week that the first train had run to the summit, not altogether satisfactorily for it had derailed. And, lo and behold, we too were brought to a stop, for the train up from Llanberis had done the very same thing. Everyone got out to inspect this interesting phenomenon and to peer down to where a distant whistle announced that the relief train was on its way. I decided not to wait but to walk back to Llanberis – yes, I was properly shod and equipped. This had two advantages: I could enjoy the sight of the little train working up the flank of the mountain, almost lost in the vastness, and I could salve that troublesome conscience. I finished up using my feet after all.

Chapter 6

Watery Themes

I have travelled far and wide in the Midlands by canal and river and, though this chapter is not about steam on the water, it was during a canal trip that I came across my first steam treat. The Ashby Canal was once a major transport route serving coal mines and ironworks. Now it is reduced to a lonely, meandering waterway which offers a leisurely weekend for the indolent as it is lock free in its somewhat truncated length. It wanders through Bosworth Field, where Richard III failed to trade England for a saddle, and arrives at the hamlet of Shackerstone. It was here that I looked across a field to an embankment on which were perched signal box, railway station and an enticing glimpse of a locomotive chimney.

I had found the Market Bosworth Light Railway, then known as the Shackerstone Railway, that has now changed its name once again to The Battlefield Line. We arrived alongside at a most propitious moment, for it was lunchtime and the local pub was a Marston's house. There was no real chance that I would have gone past without sniffing around the old line, but at least I had an excuse ready for the other passengers. It turned out to be the day when my wife and I both fell for the station museum, and we have been coming back ever since. I hope that at the end of this brief description the reader will understand why.

This is a railway which, in many ways, epitomises the amateur approach, in the best sense of that word. It is run on love, goodwill and not a lot of money. Bumbling along very nicely, with a history of eccentricities, it somehow works. It is, like the Bluebell, very much a branch line, but one which developed by default rather than from an overbearing

passion to see a railway built in this now peacefully rural corner of the country.

The story begins in the manic years of the 1840s, when it was believed that railways were a road to instant profits. Schemes of all sorts were rushed forward and the Gullivers of the first railway boom felt themselves in increasing danger of being tied down by hordes of Lilliputians. Several new schemes threatened the Midland monopoly on the lines that served the Leicestershire coalfields, the area also served by the old Ashby Canal. So the Midland bought up the Ashby, which they did not really want, and proposed a new line for the area to join Burton-on-Trent to Nuneaton – which they did not much want either. It was with great relief that they watched the rival schemes die away and, although they were stuck with the canal, the railway plan was promptly shelved. However, the coalfield was still a rich area and eventually a new proposal emerged, this time from the mighty London and North Western Railway (LNWR), the Midland's great rival. The Midland at once developed new enthusiasm for their old plan, but were less enthusiastic about finding the cash for it. Neither company was really keen on the line, but neither wanted the other to build it. The way was open for that most British of solutions, a compromise.

Agreement was reached in 1867 for the construction of the Ashby and Nuneaton Joint Railway by the Midland and LNWR. It did not have the most propitious of beginnings. Construction was slow, to say the least; first, the workforce was gathered but there were no building materials, then when the materials arrived it was harvest time and the men went off to the farms. It was supposed to take two years to build and took four; estimates were for

£172,000 and it cost over half a million. An extra branch line was completed – rails, signals, the lot – and no train was ever hauled along it from the day it opened to the day it closed. In spite of the fact that no one really wanted the main line, it did well enough for a time. Freight was its lifeblood and the passenger service dropped away so rapidly that it closed in 1931, apart from special excursions. Goods traffic kept it going for a long while, but it finally succumbed in 1970.

It seems to be the fate of this line to exist by default. It would have been just another dead branch line if local enthusiasts had not been looking for a home for a locomotive. It was grandly named *The King* but was scarcely of regal dimensions, a little 0-4-0 well tank of 1906, which spent its working life in the glassworks of St Helens. But if you have a locomotive, you need somewhere to keep it, and if you are going to keep it, you want to run it. So the Shackerstone Railway Society was born and track was acquired from Shackerstone to Market Bosworth. Few people had heard of

Shackerstone until the Market Bosworth Railway appeared and the rejuvenated *King* puffed off to pay his respects to the long dead king of Bosworth Field.

For a line built to serve collieries and ironworks, it has not been short of royal connections. George VI zoomed through on one of his war-time tours, but the railway's moment of glory came – or should have come – with the arrival of Edward VII. No efforts were spared to make the visit a success: the company built a raised section and covered it with red carpet so that His Majesty could step straight from the carriage on to the platform. Crowds gathered in the fields and stood all down the tree-lined drive that led from the station towards Gopsall Hall, where the King was intending to spend a weekend slaughtering the local wildlife. At first all went well. The driver stopped with immaculate timing so that royal carriage door stood opposite the royal raised platform. But someone had blundered: the platform was too high. Entourage pushed, porters pulled but royal door remained jammed. There was

The locomotive *The King* on the Shackerstone Railway, its name still covered by the Union Jack as it waits for the naming ceremony. The engine now has a new home on the Ribble Railway. (Anthony Burton)

nothing for it but to move the train and let the King clamber down on to uncarpeted stone. Like one of his predecessors on the throne, he was not amused. He swept from the train to closed car and the crowds didn't see him at all.

The King has long gone and even Gopsall Hall is no more. But the tree-lined drive and the station remain, and a bump on the platform can just be discerned. Shackerstone Station has a delightful situation and though the busy times when it stood at the junction of the freight lines to Moira and Coalville have gone, it remains a place to enchant those who find romance in railway history. It is, as I said, home to a quite splendid museum. There are two basic approaches to museums, which one might call those of the peacocks and those of the squirrels: the one concentrating on brilliant display, the other on hoarding up all manner of goodies. This is a squirrel museum. It is a collection put together by John Jacques, a British Rail signalman from a railway family.

It all began thirty years ago, when the old semaphore signals, illuminated by oil lamps and worked through mechanical links to levers in the signal box, began to disappear in favour of electric lights. No one seemed especially interested in the discards, so John began taking them in and then kept on collecting: old photographs, signs, timetables, posters, uniforms, tickets, lanterns, in fact anything connected with the railway but with a special emphasis on Shackerstone where he had worked as a lad. Everything somehow gets fitted in, every inch of wall is covered, every ledge, table and corner filled. There is just about room for visitors and it looks as though he is squirrelling away still. Good luck to him, for it is a wonderful collection to browse through, with each visit unearthing a new gem. There may be a logical sequence to the display, but it escaped my notice and I really do not care, because order would be a poor substitute for the delights of browsing and discovery.

Shackerstone Station may once have been a junction but its appearance remains that of a stopping-off place on a rural line. It is surrounded by peaceful,

A black and white photograph of the lovely little museum at Shackerstone, included because it shows the late John Jacques who put much of this collection together. (Anthony Burton)

gentle countryside with small fields still bounded by hedges, for this part of the Midlands has mercifully not yet been invaded by prairie farming. The canal winds through, an artificial waterway but one so convoluted that it has all the appearance of a natural stream. There is nothing dramatic here, not even on the railway itself, which has that air of quiet efficiency which was once the hallmark of the Midland. Brass gleams in the nearby signal box, the track is in fair order and a motley array of locomotives and rolling stock is on view. There is one BR Class 4 but the rest are the mixture of Bagnells, Pecketts and Hunslets you would expect to find, ruled over, of course, by the *King*. Coaching stock has some oddities on show. There are some standard coaches, but there are also a couple of converted diesel units which served their working lives as a viaduct inspection train and a griddle car. The latter really is an oddity, a sort of cross between an American observation car and a mobile cocktail bar. The design was devised at Doncaster to herald a new age of British Rail luxury, but they were not popular and only half a dozen or so were built. This survivor brings a note of grace to the Market Bosworth Railway.

The journey is pleasing and peaceful with frequent glimpses of the canal and the sort of scenery that seems almost too good to be true. Trees and hedges, fields and lanes, seem to have been set in order to satisfy the demands of country calendar designers. It is never dull, and nor is life on the footplate. The route from Shackerstone begins with a stiff gradient. There is scarcely time to collect the token from the signal box before the hard work starts, and twenty pounds of pressure have slipped down the gauge before the fireman has time to pick up his shovel. So a great deal of coal has to be spread around the box before anyone can relax. Then there is a gentle trundle before the downhill run to Market Bosworth which, the fireman duly notes, means another

start on an uphill grade for the return journey.

Market Bosworth is well worth exploring and, until recently, could boast of having the Hoskins' Brewery's only tied house. The Red Lion has now been joined by a couple of others but remains a good, honest, friendly pub. The pub is still there but Hoskins Brewery is sadly no longer with us. You will probably welcome a pint, for the town stands on top of a hill and the railway is at the bottom and it is a good long walk, which goes some way to explain the lack of enthusiasm for railway travel among the local populace. The change is symbolised at the station, now – ultimate indignity – a garage, though there are still facilities for rail passengers. Plans are well advanced for an extension of the line to Bosworth Field and the battle site, which would link the railway to a popular tourist spot. This has now been achieved and the line given a catchy new name – The Battlefield Line. Making suitable links is one way of making a railway pay. The Market Bosworth line is unlikely to become one of the top ten tourist attractions in Britain and there will always be some who dismiss it as big boys trying to be little boys playing at trains. It is not, in fact, a male preserve at all but, even so, why not? The railway society members get a great deal of satisfaction and pleasure from the line, give a great deal of pleasure to others, and are preserving something which will give pleasure for generations to come. Bravo the amateurs, say I, not a view always shared by the professionals of the big, successful, preserved lines.

Michael Draper, general manager and financial director of the Severn Valley Railway, has no doubt that they are part of the leisure industry. He runs a business with a turnover of a million and a half a year and he, and the shareholders, expect it to show a profit. He is not noticeably reticent in propounding his views on how a railway should be run and, as far as organisation is concerned, the Market Bosworth and the Severn Valley could scarcely show a greater contrast.

Profitability and efficiency are the key words on the Severn, even if the product being sold is essentially the same: steam and nostalgia. It is the emphasis which changes. Steam and nostalgia would certainly be the running order for the Market Bosworth Railway, but nostalgia and steam would, I suspect, be more likely on the Severn Valley. For every steam buff who turns up, there are a dozen families out for an old-fashioned railway trip, in which steam is just one element. But you cannot take that element away, for it is the steam train buffs who keep the enterprise going. The Railway Society has over 13,000 members who provide tangible support; they are, in fact, mainly responsible for running the trains. The permanent staff control the organisation and, when necessary, step in to take on any job that needs doing, but drivers and firemen, guards and porters on the Severn Valley are there, as on most preserved lines, for the love of it. Why is it so successful in attracting members? The answer is to be found in those three famous initials: GWR.

This was, indeed, once part of the Great Western empire, though it had a period of some twenty years' independence before being swallowed whole in the 1870s. It was never a very important line: four trains up, four trains down was the usual allocation for passengers, and there was some freight traffic serving the local farming community and Alveley Colliery. It followed a familiar pattern of declining fortunes, culminating in closure during the Beeching era – at which point enter the volunteers. The story is the same as for other preserved lines, but would it have been preserved without those three magic initials? Possibly. Would it have been preserved in its present form? I doubt it. Stop any enthusiasts near the line and ask for a description of a typical train, and like as not they will describe a dark green

locomotive, hauling a train made up of coaches painted in chocolate and cream. Then, when the next train duly appears as a red LMS or a black BR loco hauling a set decorated in what is officially known as crimson and cream, but more popularly as blood and custard, they will be suitably astonished. Chances are, however, that the set after that will be as they described and confidence will be restored.

Not everything is GWR, but enough to make that the dominant feature. It is an image assiduously cultivated at the stations, in platform furniture, old posters and assorted insignia. It also runs over into operations, where signalling was, until recently, exclusively Great Western in style. The pattern appeared to have been broken on the new extension to Kidderminster when a modern, suburban-type electrical system was shown in the pages of the Society's magazine. Keen-eyed readers, however, soon spotted the date in the corner of the plan – 1 April 1986. Tradition will not easily be ousted, for that is what the customers are paying to see. And, by customers, I am not referring just to the families who turn up every day throughout the summer, but to all the excursion bookings, the dining-out specials and the lucrative hiring by film and television companies. Reliving the past is a major part of the appeal, and the profit, of the Severn Valley Railway.

If this were all the Severn Valley had to offer, it would be just one more in a succession of lines; but it does have that bit extra. It offers a good length of track, sixteen miles in all, which means long trains and comparatively large locomotives. And success breeds success. Because it is a popular line with a quite outstanding collection of locomotives, they can afford to indulge in exchanges. There are no fewer than sixteen GWR engines, including those great favourites of the enthusiast, the Manors and the Halls, and, rather surprisingly, almost as many LMS, ten of them, including Jubilee-class *Leander* and *Galatea*. When these engines go out on loan, others come in to take their place, so there is always a chance of finding something rather special on hand when you stop by. I had not checked up in advance of my visit but it turned out that luck was with me for there, waiting in the sidings at Bridgnorth, was *City of Truro.*

This locomotive is one of a select body known not just as representatives of a class but as stars in their own right. The story dates back to the end of the last century when the reputation of GWR Swindon-built locomotives was at something of a low ebb. The chief engineer, William Dean, had a new assistant, George Jackson Churchward, the man who was to give true distinction to the railway in many ways. Between them they began planning a new class of locomotives with big 6-foot 8-inch-diameter coupled driving wheels and – what was to become Churchward's hallmark – long tapering boilers. Dean retired and when the new engines appeared Churchward was the man in charge. They were all called after cities served by the railway, *City of Truro* among them. There was nothing in the engine itself to distinguish it from others of the class, but it happened to be the locomotive that was heading the Ocean Mail from Plymouth to Paddington on 9 May 1904. The train reached Wellington Bank and with everything opened wide it thundered down at a speed recorded as 102.3 mph. It was the first time the magic 100-miles-per-hour figure had been passed. Experts are still arguing about the accuracy of the recorded speed, but you will never convince a GWR enthusiast to the contrary.

And there she stood in Bridgnorth, as bright and sparkling as when she set out on that world record run more than eighty years ago. Eighty years old – it simply does not seem possible, because the engine does not look its age. It looks exactly what it is: not a locomotive that marked the end of the Victorian era,

but one that sounded the arrival of the twentieth century.

It was a busy day at Bridgnorth, but not many came to look at the old lady. To the majority of visitors it was just another steam locomotive like the others running on the line or standing at sidings or in the shed. But there were a few who could not drag themselves away from it. They walked around it, bent to look at the mechanism of valves and cylinders, but mostly just stood in admiration of the whole. It did not look, in truth, a sprinter, like the famous streamlined A4 Pacific *Mallard* which grabbed and held the world record for the LNER, but it looked wonderfully strong. To the steam agnostic, the non-believer, it is absurd to suggest that an engine has a character of its own. Well, *City of Truro* has. It starts with the frame, the great square metal plates on which the boiler rests and around which all the moving parts of pistons and valve gears are located. It is very prominent, a rigid, solid structure around the wheels, and it is very reassuring. Nothing, you feel, is going to fall apart here if we let rip. The frame will stand it. Up above there is a glimpse of elegance and a touch of the thoroughbred in the boiler, tapering down from the bulging firebox, the heart of the engine. And she was born when a lady was expected to look her best on all occasions, so immaculate paintwork emphasises shapeliness, in delicate lines traced over the prevailing green. If the *City of Truro* fails to give you a thrill, do not bother with the rest of the steam world.

The day was not to be crowned with a ride behind the old record-breaker. Instead, we were handed over to the LMS, to the ministrations of a heavy freight engine: no greyhound this, but a solid, hardworking, powerful beast. Passenger trains may be the glamorous end of railway life, but companies looked to freight for a steady, reliable income which depended on steady, reliable locomotives. Sir William Stanier set out to provide just that and the first of his new locomotives rolled out of the works in 1935. No class or locomotive names here; our engine was a plain 8F number 8233, a number which must have been recorded in thousands of schoolboy notebooks since it first left Glasgow in 1940. You might think that this would detract from the GWR flavour but once you are sat in your train what you see is not so much your own workhorse as the others out on the line, so the view through my carriage window was all Great Western. There was, in any case, atmosphere and other more tangible things to be absorbed first. A feature of all the Severn Valley stations is the effort that has been made to create an image reminiscent of the line's heyday. It was an age when travellers arrived with mountainous piles of luggage, when stations had more flowers on display than the municipal park, and when plastic suggested something that could be moved rather than a material mass-produced to make one station look like another. That seems to me to be the crucial difference between this renovation and the modern equivalent: materials like stone, wood and iron give both a sense of place and

Former GWR locomotive *Odney Manor* running alongside the River Severn on the Severn Valley Railway. (Lewis Maddox)

individuality. The rough stone blocks of the main building contrast with the intricate ironwork on the footbridge and the even more elaborate work on the cast-iron urinal on the platform. This, perhaps, comes a little too soon in the account. Male passengers are more likely to encounter it after a visit to the Railwayman's Arms, once the plain refreshment room and now the railway pub, noted for offering a variety of different beers. On offer was the genuine black country brew of Batham's and, a newcomer to me, Titanic Ale. You read the name out loud and the barman waits with the long-suffering air of one who knows that he is about to hear a witticism he has encountered a thousand times before. 'Gives you a sinking feeling does it?' The crowd at the bar duly laughs. He knows he has kept the best line for himself: 'Goes down well with ice.' I stuck with Batham's, then went off to inspect the cast iron on Platform 2.

Once you set out on the journey you realise that the name Severn Valley is entirely apt, for the river is a constant companion all the way to Bewdley. Restoration of historical routes is a

curious business. Here we were travelling on a hundred-year-old railway which is back running a service more successfully than it has ever done before, and part of its charm and its success lies with the scenery: in the view of the quiet, peacefully winding river. A coach party on a works' outing from Coventry had joined the train and they exclaimed over the beauty of the countryside, delighted to get away from the industrial heart of the Midlands. Yet the Severn was once the country's primary trading route, the King's Highway. On its banks the great Darby ironworks ushered in the industrial world; across it went the world's first iron bridge, and on its waters the trade of the nation was carried on a variety of barges, including the old Severn trows. They traded not just to Bridgnorth but farther upstream to Ironbridge and Shrewsbury. Now nothing much bigger than a canoe can pass this way. Railway trade did for the river trade, but perhaps just as railway trade declined and reappeared in new form, so the Severn may thrive again. I should dearly love to look down from my train to see a barge under sail, and I should be equally pleased to turn from the tiller to wave to the driver of a passing Hall.

Pulling out of the station on the road south you get a good view over Bridgnorth town, or towns since it is divided into two parts, High and Low. The distinction is physical rather than social and the two parts are still joined by a cliff railway. It is almost as old as our line, having been completed in 1892 when it worked on the water-balance principle. If you want to know how it operated, I suggest listening to Gerard Hoffnung's account of life on a building site. 'As I was going up I met the bucket coming down' is as good a description as any of a water balance. It now runs on electricity but is still good fun, and a great saving on the legs. You can also see the first of the sandstone cliffs which are a prominent feature of the whole run, and which help

to establish both the natural characteristics of the area and the nature of its buildings. The stone can be seen in the precariously leaning ruin of the old castle. Bridgnorth was, until recently, a town whose streets were clogged by traffic but a new bypass road has helped enormously, and given the railway a new feature: a concrete viaduct. The old railway viaducts used to be instantly recognisable from the road, but this modern structure looks so like a flyover that it comes as a shock to motorists on the bypass to find a large steam locomotive puffing across over their heads.

The line does not pass through the easiest of country for railway builders. It is full of dips and hollows, lumps and bumps. You start with a high embankment which gives way to a five-arched viaduct, a rather grand structure for such a minor line, but initially there were plans for a route to Wolverhampton. The viaduct is all that remains of what might have been. The line climbs continuously, the engine working ever harder while the hill seems to be getting ever steeper; then it reaches a point where the engineers seemed to have abandoned hope of going over the hill, and went through it instead. A short tunnel leads to a deep sandstone cutting, the side still bearing the scars of blast holes and pick marks. Then the summit is reached and the footplate men can take a breather for a mile and a half of downhill running.

The river is only ever half a mile away at the most, so that it is very much the dominant theme in the scenery. Swans drift through the green strands of weeds which flow and wave in the current. The banks sprout anglers' umbrellas like technicolour fungi. There is even a special variety of river architecture: rows of little wooden huts, no two alike; simple structures for families who want to have a day out on the river. The watery theme continues later when the line runs past reservoirs which on sunny, breezy week-ends bear a mass of tacking dinghies.

A watermill reminds us that the river was once a source of industrial power; a caravan park that it is now mainly providing a background for leisure activities. But among all the riverside structures, the railway more than holds its own, and you will find few structures as attractive as the Severn Valley stations.

Hampton Loade is the first stop and if you thought that Bridgnorth seemed to epitomise the old-style delights of the country railway, then just wait until you see the other stations along the line. There is the same rich stone but an even greater profusion of flowers, more signs and posters, barrows piled still higher with leather trunks or shiny milk churns. Stations were originally designed to attract travellers, but on a sunny day these stations seem to lure you away with promises of green fields and poppies among the corn. And if you do get off, this is as good a place as any to alight. You can wander down to the river, sup a pint at the Unicorn and, if that does not take your fancy, wander down to the ferry, cross the river and try the Lion on the opposite bank. After that comes Highley, but between there is a place which was once one of the most important stops on the line, though you might not think so now. Alveley was the nearest point to the colliery, but you have to look hard today to see evidence that it ever existed at all. The countryside between Hampton Loade and Highley seems as pleasantly rural as any you meet along the way.

If you like your stations quaint and folksy with just a touch of the dramatic, you cannot beat Arley. You can look across to the little crenellated church on the hill or admire the deep cutting through the sandstone which will lead you to the most famous feature on the whole line. The track begins to curve round to meet the river and you catch a glimpse of the single, elegant arch which will carry you across the water. When it was built in 1861, the Victoria Bridge was the widest iron arch in the world. It is interesting to see just how far technology has moved on since that first iron bridge was built across the Severn at Ironbridge in 1777. That was a complex jigsaw of small sections, assembled just as a woodworker would assemble them in a series of dovetail and mortice joints. Here everything has been simplified to one smooth elliptical span, a graceful curve on which rests the horizontal platform of the railway. Not that you see much of that as you go across, for this really is a place where the spectator gets the best of the game; more than once I have waited here listening for the distant snorting which announces the arrival of the train that will complete the scene. I usually keep my fingers crossed in the hope that there will be a spectacular locomotive at the head. Goodness knows how many photographs have been taken here and how many times the bridge has featured on television and film.

I am equally attached to the approach to Bewdley, if only because the town itself is packed with interest and much of its character can be appreciated as the train pulls in towards the station. You get advance warning when you see the viaduct off to the west, which once carried the line from Bewdley to Cleobury Mortimer. There is a rather poignant little railway tale about Cleobury Mortimer. It was once the terminus of the grandly named Cleobury Mortimer and Ditton Priors Light Railway. When the last passenger train ran in 1938, so many enthusiasts turned up for the last rites that the service was delayed. On into the night went the little train, gas lights twinkling, and then the gas ran out and the last train ran on in total darkness. Happily the lights do not look like going out on the Severn Valley.

Other sights along the way produce mixed emotions: delight at the old watermill, a less ecstatic welcome for the caravan park by the river. Then on to Bewdley and a dramatic entrance to the town which was once a major inland port.

Small Prairie tank steaming over a viaduct on the Severn Valley Railway. (Lewis Maddox)

The route takes us above the rooftops, above the ropewalk where yarn was twisted to moor and bowhaul the river's barges, high too above the bridge built by Thomas Telford to carry the road across the Severn. Everything tells you that this is a town to savour and enjoy.

Until recently, Bewdley was the end of the line, but in the summer of 1984 the first passenger train steamed through Bewdley on its way to Kidderminster. For the Severn Valley this was an expensive addition to the track, but one which held out hopes of future profits. Like the proposed extension of the Bluebell to East Grinstead, it was designed to link into the British Rail network. However, it takes the traveller out of the true Severn Valley into odd, exotic locations. Up to this point the atmosphere might be described as romanticised English rural, but now a foreign element comes into this cosy world. Geese and pigs, cows and ducks, give way to llamas and bison, deer and antelope, for the line runs past the fringes of the West Midlands Safari Park. It is an odd experience, akin to boating through London Zoo on the Regent's Canal. It certainly breaks the calm nostalgia of the rest of the line, but this returns later in the brand new station at Kidderminster. The foreign wildlife gives way again to a very English scene, less romantic than the woods and fields of the Severn Valley, but no less typical. The line crosses the little River Stour and the lovely Staffs and Worcester Canal, while from the viaduct you look out over a landscape reminiscent of the industrial revolution. The horizon is punctuated by the exclamation marks of mill chimneys, for this was once a major centre for carpet manufacture. The station at Kidderminster, new in date but traditional in style, is well able to stand comparison with its Victorian neighbours down the line. It is a model of how traditional style and modern materials can be combined satisfactorily, and is a credit to the railway.

You come away from the Severn Valley Line feeling that you have had a thoroughly English day out. But not everyone hankers after this sort of home-grown pleasure, so for those who are looking for something completely different I recommend the Nene Valley Railway. Not that the valley of the Nene has anything foreign about it: quite the contrary. If anything, it is even more redolent of English atmosphere – one part *Three Men in a Boat* and two parts *Wind in the Willows* – which characterises the loveliest waterways. The river meanders through meadows, past little villages often graced by surprisingly grand churches; and, above all, it offers peace. Where the Thames is full of people dashing about, the Nene is the preserve of messers about in boats.

So one might expect the Nene Valley Railway to match or surpass the Severn Valley for quaintness and general nostalgia. It doesn't even try. Instead it presents a world wholly alien to most railway enthusiasts in this country. Its speciality is its international flavour. Where a knowledgeable visitor to the Severn takes pleasure in the sight of *Hagley Hall* heading a rake of chocolate and cream coaches, one would have to look hard to make out what was coming around the bend on this line. Only the very, very knowledgeable could say with certainty, 'Ah, yes, that's a Swedish A20 with a French set.' But it did not start out like that.

The story begins, as at Market Bosworth, with a locomotive and, as so often before, with one man's enthusiasm. The Reverend Richard Paten was in love with steam railways and his own local line in particular, and concerned that its long history should not go unremarked. The Northampton to Peterborough line had been surveyed by the great George Stephenson himself. It opened in 1845 and was soon joined to other major trunk routes, including the main line from King's Cross. But while the latter prospered, the original went into decline and seemed doomed for closure. The age of steam was coming to an end, and though many mourned its passing, few were willing or able to do anything about it. Richard Paten, however, was determined to save something from the wreckage, so he bought one of the locomotives he had often seen steaming through Peterborough, a BR Standard Class 5, No. 73050, which he hoped to display permanently as a monument to the steam age. He found it to be in remarkably good condition, and to have followed his original plan would have been akin to sending a pet dog alive to the taxidermist. He gave 73050 a name – *City of Peterborough* – and a society was formed to bring the engine back to life. All that was needed was somewhere to run it, and, of course, money.

For once the timing was excellent. The old Nene Valley Line was closed and available. Peterborough was undergoing massive changes, having been accorded new town status, a weird notion for a cathedral city that can trace its origins to a monastic foundation of the seventh century. There were plans for it to double in size, and the new development corporation was hunting for ways to add to Peterborough's appeal. If you want industrialists to move in, you have to have something more to offer than

a bare site. Moving a business means moving people and people like to think they are coming to a place of character. So why not add a steam railway to the attractions, a steam railway unlike any other in Britain?

It was the very dereliction of the old line that made it possible. Almost everything had to be done from scratch. Trains are limited as to where they can go by the loading gauge: you cannot have carriages crashing into platform edges or scraping against tunnel walls, and the European loading gauge is more generous than the British. But there was nothing to stop the amateur navvies of the Nene Valley rebuilding to the extended gauge, and as one of the members wanted to buy a big Swedish locomotive and run it on the line, there was every reason to do so. The notion was born that the Nene Valley Railway would be genuinely European, with continental and British locomotives and rolling stock running side by side. It is an instructive, perhaps bizarre, spectacle, and one which does not appeal to all tastes. When it comes to theories of railway design, your average British enthusiast makes Alf Garnett look like an internationalist. Here one can make direct comparisons and put prejudices to the test, and the truly xenophobic can see the benighted foreigners without having to leave the country.

A British Railways Class 5 locomotive, *City of Peterborough*, crossing the River Nene on the Nene Valley Railway. (Nene Valley Railway)

The Nene Valley Railway is undoubtedly an object lesson in different approaches to locomotive design. You could not ask for greater contrast than that provided by the Battle of Britain class, with its air-smoothed boiler giving it a clean and somewhat slabby appearance. German locomotives have the motion out on display and the boiler is festooned with curling pipes. It looks like a mobile central heating system – a phrase which I borrow from a volunteer working on the Nene. It is a phrase which seems to sum up the British attitude: fascination with the different, foreign approach but a lurking suspicion that this is not the way things should be done. Rolling stock too comes from all over the place, so that any one train can present an odd mixture of styles. I travelled in a set of French coaches hauled by a very English workhorse, a Hunslet Austerity.

The coaches were comfortable but unmistakably foreign. The windows were TV-screen shaped, giving the strange impression that the scenery outside was back-projected, which it often is on this line, because the presence of so much European stock has made it a popular place with film-makers. The Nene has featured in all kinds of films, from television's *Secret Army* to a James Bond epic. Like their old British counterparts, the French railways advertised places that could be visited along the line, such as Haute Savoie and Auxerre instead of the Wye Valley and Blackpool. There was a reminder that in Europe trains crossed frontiers: the notice by the window said *Alarme – Notbremse – Freno d'Emergen-zia – Alarm*. My one criticism was that the doors were hinged instead of sliding, so that every time you left the compartment you blocked the corridor.

Strictly speaking this photo has no place in a book on steam, but this Swedish railcar is such an unusual member of the Nene Valley European collection, it seemed a shame to leave it out. (Nene Valley Railway)

Papplewick pumping station could easily be mistaken for a rather eccentric Victorian country house in its attractive setting. (Anthony Burton)

The journey began at the old Northampton and Peterborough Railway Station at Wansford which, appropriately enough, has something of a continental air with its prominent Dutch gables. It has been joined on site by Branwell Station from down the line. While there is plenty of space for humans, the hardware has to huddle together outside: row upon row of engines, a European Community of steam. The journey, like that on the Severn Valley line, is very much a river trip, with two crossings over water and views of river features such as the guillotine lock – so called because the gates lift vertically, which is alarming when you go under in a boat – and the watermill at Caster. The scenery has an odd look about it, which is disconcerting until you realise the scale of man's intervention. The new town corporation, looking to make the most of the surrounding countryside, has created Nene Park, rearranging the landscape to meet the needs of golfers and joggers, fishermen and caravanners. It looks contrived and I cannot say that I care for

it. The main excitement for the younger passengers came with the 616-yard-long tunnel, and the kids screamed their heads off all the way through. It produces a most satisfactory, deafening racket.

Our journey ended at the smart new station at Orton Mere, but the extension to Peterborough itself was all but complete and awaited only the official benediction of a royal opening. So by now the citizens of Peterborough will have found the 125s of the main line joined by all manner of *exotica* steaming up the Nene valley.

Having gone on a bit about the neat and not gaudy appearance of British engineering, I could not leave this part of the Midlands without crossing into Nottinghamshire and visiting the most elaborate, extraordinary and delightful steam location in the country. Although Papplewick Pumping Station may not be a name which immediately sets the pulse racing, it stands as a monument not only to the steam age, but to the romantic notions in the hearts of many outwardly sober dignitaries of the Victorian era.

If you approach the site without knowing what the building houses, you could be excused a certain bewilderment. The first thing you see is a lake surrounded by ornamental shrubs which appears to belong to a fine garden in the French style, a sort of Nottingham Versailles. Beyond that is a building of no obvious style at all, best described as a cross between a nonconformist chapel and a Transylvanian castle. Only the tall chimney in the background gives the game away. This is no chapel but a temple of steam. The magic lies inside.

Walk round the pond with its scalloped stone edges, climb the steps of the main building beneath the elaborate porch, push open the massive and beautiful wooden doors and Papplewick engine house is revealed in its glory.

Now, suppose you were a civic dignitary in Nottingham in the 1880s. The Corporation Water Department has voted the sum of £51,000 for a new pumping station to lift three million gallons of water a day from deep wells and serve the needs of the growing city. You are proud of this new technological wonder and you wish to dignify it with an appropriate architectural setting. The pumping station is miles from anywhere and few of the good citizens are likely to come to see it. Does that deter you? Certainly not. So you go to your engineer, M. Ogle Tarbotton Esquire, and tell him to give of his best. Give of his best Mr Tarbotton assuredly did.

An engine house has certain basic requirements: it needs to be a solid building, not simply because it needs to protect the engine from the weather, but to provide a solid frame to hold the movements of big, heavy engine parts. So it will contain strengthening columns which can also act as the engine frame. The building also needs light for the engine men to work in. In bald outline that describes the building, but when it came to providing that extra touch of decoration the whole place was transformed. A waterworks, it was decided, should have watery themes, so the windows, all different, were glorified

Papplewick is noted not only for its magnificent beam engines but also for its ornate interior with brightwork decorated pillars and stained glass windows). (Anthony Burton)

by stained glass depicting water plants. Then there were the supporting columns. Each is covered in a tracery of bright metal with metal fish swimming through metal reeds and, at the very top, instead of plain capitals, four ibis stand, one at each corner of the square column. In the middle of all this splendour are two huge beam engines by James Watt and Company, replete with gleaming brass and mahogany.

The whole effect is one of sumptuous splendour, so grand it scarcely seems possible that all this exists for something as mundane as providing water for a wash basin in Nottingham. But that is the whole point: the decoration is a visual expression of pride in important work well done. Part of the appeal is recognition of the function behind the elaboration. The ornate pond supplies cooling water for the condenser; the decorated columns take the stresses from the rocking-beams. And if you really want to get in touch with raw reality, you can wander to the back of the engine house to find the bank of Lancashire boilers, which in working days consumed 2,000 tons of coal a year. Now the giants are steamed only on special weekends, and then the whole place comes to life. The ornate decoration can be seen as a perfect foil to the weighty but precisely elegant motion of the great machines. One can use a much misused word without fear of contradiction: Papplewick is unique.

Chapter 7

The Rally

Papplewick Pumping Station may be unique, but it does not represent the complete Papplewick steam story, a fact I discovered on a typical August weekend of howling winds and massing dark clouds. Adding to the darkness was the black smoke from a collection of some forty grand engines, among them a Ruston Proctor steamroller of 1915, its beautiful paintwork proclaiming the ownership of H & B Palmer of Papplewick. The event was the annual Cromford Steam Rally, a display of agricultural engines, showman's engines, rollers, tractors, wagons and just about anything that moved by steam but was not designed to run on rails. And, as the traction engine fraternity were happy to point out, steam engines were seen on the roads before they appeared on the railways.

The story of the steam engine on the roads of Britain goes back 200 years. It begins with William Murdock, an assistant to James Watt, who was working down in Cornwall on the big pumping engines. He designed a small steam carriage, worked by a high-pressure engine. He was delighted with the results, but the boss was furious. Watt, who had shown his disapproval of high-pressure pumping engines, was even less pleased at the idea of high-pressure moving engines. Experimentation thus came to an end and was revived only with the expiry of the Watt patent in 1800, at which point the maverick figure of Richard Trevithick appeared. Before he began work on his railway locomotive, he built a successful steam carriage; but, in typical Trevithick fashion, he repaired to a local hostelry to celebrate with friends, leaving the new machine simmering outside. Pressure built up and a loud explosion announced

the end of Trevithick's first engine.

Subsequent models showed that the steam carriage was a practical proposition, but it soon fell foul of authority. Huge road tolls were levied so the steam men turned to the railroads where their engines could run untroubled by tolls and other vehicles. It is interesting to note that what are generally regarded as the first successful attempts to produce road transport based on the internal combustion engine began with Karl Benz in 1885, almost exactly a hundred years after Murdock. How might things have changed had the steam men had a free hand to work on their ideas? Like all historical 'ifs', the question cannot be answered, but it gives rise to interesting speculation.

The movement back to the road began down on the farm. The idea of a portable steam engine which would provide power for activities such as threshing was very attractive. Such an engine was demonstrated at an agricultural show at Wrangle in Lincolnshire in 1837. Others took up the idea, but it was not until 1845 that construction began on a commercial scale. Over the next ten years the engineering firm of Clayton and Shuttleworth built more than 2,000 of these engines. Not everyone was impressed. Thomas Aveling of Cambridgeshire looked at the portable engine and remarked scathingly that 'it is an insult to mechanical science to see half a dozen horses drag along a steam engine, and the sight of six sailing vessels towing a steamer would certainly not be more ridiculous.'

He was, of course, quite right: all over the country steam locomotives were dashing around pulling heavy loads, so why not adapt the portable engine so that it could move itself? This is just what Aveling did, adding a simple gearing and a chain drive to a standard Clayton and Shuttleworth engine. However, it still had to have a horse in front, not to pull it but because there was no other method of steering. This was obviously unsatisfactory and in time steering systems were introduced. The traction engine had arrived.

There was still a problem about moving a traction engine from place to place, for they were restricted by the notorious Red Flag Act of 1865. This said that an engine could travel on the road only if a man walked sixty yards in front with a flag to warn of the approach of the steam monster. The red flag disappeared in 1878, but the man in front remained until 1896, as did a whole set of other regulations, making journeys by road slow and hideously expensive.

It says a lot for the advantages bestowed by these engines that farmers were willing to put up with the expense and inconvenience and began to ask for new ways of using steam on the land. Ploughing was an obvious candidate but one which presented great problems. Steam engines were vast and heavy, and an engine would have flattened the ground, compacting it so hard that the following plough could not cut through it. The solution to the problem came from John Fowler in the 1850s and established what was to become a standard method for steam ploughing. In 1858 he was awarded a prize of £500 at the Royal Agricultural Show for producing the first economical steam plough. The new design had a big, powerful engine situated at either side of the field, each fitted with a winding drum holding a wire rope which passed from one to the other. A plough was attached to the rope and was then hauled across the field. The two engines could then be moved forward and the plough would be hauled back to dig the next furrow, and so on down the field. The use of two big engines involved great expense, so steam ploughing was reserved for the big farms. The small farmer went on with his team of horses until the arrival of the tractor in the twentieth century.

An important feature in the life of town and country was the fair, which began as a specialist occasion for selling sheep, cattle and horses or for the annual hiring of labour. It was a time for business but it was also a time for fun, and the fun side increasingly depended on the travelling showmen who went around the country with their collections of booths and rides. The successful fair is brash, bright and noisy. A restrained, polite fair is unthinkable. So for the showman, anything that could add to the general noise and brilliance was welcome, and the invention of the electric light bulb seemed to have been made just for his benefit. Unfortunately, in the early days, this meant taking around hundreds of big, heavy batteries to provide power. Then Faraday discovered the principles of electro-magnetism and the dynamo, and the generator appeared. And what was needed to turn a dynamo? A steam engine, of course.

Traction engine inventor Aveling was among the leading manufacturers to produce dual-purpose engines for showmen. They could haul the fairground wagons from site to site, and, once in position, could turn the night-time fair into a brilliant display of colour and light. A Burrell catalogue of 1909 shows one of their engines hauling a train of five wagons, each labelled 'Hancock's Great West of England Steam Switchback', and because the engines were as much on display as the rides they powered and the lights they lit, they too had to be brilliant and garish. There was a profusion of brass and copper, elaborate paintwork and a canopy often supported on twisted 'barley sugar' columns. These were the racy, raffish end of the steam world, with each engine having its own personality and its own name.

Out on the roads, progress was hampered by the restrictive legislation and, to some extent, by the appalling roads themselves. Steam was to help sort this out. The road works' sign today brings only a groan from the motorist who sees the tail end of a traffic jam coming up before him. As a child, the sign for me meant the excitement of seeing a steamroller, and if you stood around long enough and asked enough questions there was usually the chance of a ride. There was also a good chance that the front of the roller carried the brass insignia of a horse rearing up on its hind legs, above the name 'Invicta'. That meant it came from the works of Thomas Aveling, for wherever you look in this part of the steam story, his name is never far away.

Better roads meant an opportunity to provide better vehicles. Removal of petty restrictions meant that for a while the steam wagon played an important role in transport. Then, in 1933, the government stepped in again. Road fund licences were revised and the cost for steam wagons was trebled, while those for petrol and diesel trucks were reduced. That, as far as road haulage was concerned, was that. The steam car had an even briefer career, but it did provide one new word for the language. The gentleman who bought such a car needed to have a competent man to look after and feed the boiler: the fireman or, in French, the *chauffeur*. Almost the last in the line of steam cars was an American model, the Doble, built in the 1920s. It had a flash boiler which could raise steam to a pressure of 750 psi in less than a minute, and this remarkable vehicle could accelerate from 0 to 40 mph in 8 seconds and had a top speed of over 100 mph. If I ever find a bottled genie who offers me the customary three wishes, one of them would be for a Doble steam sports car.

This, then, is a potted history of steam on the road and on the land and it may give some idea of what you might expect to find at a steam rally. But everything we have looked at so far has been tied to the working world, even the glamorous showman's engines. Indeed, the latter were among the hardest worked of all engines. They had to pull heavy loads from site to site and when they reached the fairground they had to continue working to supply power. So how, where, and when did the engines make the transition from workhorses to show horses? These are questions that can be answered with some accuracy.

By the end of the 1940s it was possible to pick up an old traction engine for little more than its scrap value and a few individuals did just that, including two friends, Arthur Napper and Miles Chetwynd-Stapylton. Napper had acquired a 1902 Marshall engine, *Old Timer,* while Chetwynd-Stapylton possessed a 1918 Aveling, *Lady Grove.* Inevitably, arguments developed over which was the better engine and, as neither would agree to accepting second best, the matter was put to the test. A half-mile course was marked out at Napper's farm at Appleton in Berkshire and the two rivals set out to race, a firkin of beer going to the winner. The private wager caught the popular imagination, and Napper thought it might be a good idea to invite other enthusiasts to bring their engines for an outing on his farm. Owners and engines gathered in the summer of 1952 for the first-ever traction engine rally. Now there are more than fifty held every year throughout Britain.

Faced by so many rallies, each having its own special characteristics, which do you choose to represent them all? The short answer is that one cannot, because all rallies have individual personalities. So I based my choice on personal whim. I chose a rally held in a spot for which I have special affection. I first visited Cromford in Derbyshire some fifteen years ago, drawn by its historic importance as the first factory town, the place where the first successful cotton-spinning mill was established. I went to look at that old mill, at the grand house built by its founder, Sir Richard Arkwright, and at the less grand houses built by Arkwright to house his workforce. I have returned time and again, and on each visit I have found some new historical aspect of the place.

I have walked the towpath of the Cromford Canal down to Leawood Pumping Station, where the 1849 beam engine that supplied water to the canal has been restored and is now regularly steamed. I have walked the Cromford and High Peak Railway, a magnificent route which takes one back to the transition period between tramway and railway, a mixture of level sections worked by locomotives and steep inclines where haulage was by stationary steam engine. One of the engine houses, Middleton Top, has been preserved and, until recently, was worked using compressed air. It was a tremendous sight, but the essential steaming ingredient was missing. Now, I am delighted to say, the great pair of engines can again be turned by genuine steam power. Add to these attractions the fact that they are to be found among superb scenery, the canal snuggling down into the bottom of the lovely Derwent Valley and the railway climbing up through the hills, and you can see why the combination is irrestistible. I would take any excuse to go back to Cromford, so the steam rally really selected itself.

One problem about visiting Cromford lies with the distractions you may meet along the way. Approaching from the north, you have to pass through Matlock Bath, home to one of the best preserved of the original Arkwright Mills. South and west offer the landscape of lead mining and the Cromford and High Peak Railway, and the west also has the charms of the Crich Tram Museum. But as none offers the concentrated delights of Cromford itself when the summer rally weekend comes round, it was not difficult to resist these siren calls. I headed

straight there and turned off the main road, making for the meadows between the River Derwent and the canal. Once on site you are plunged into the heart of the event, for steam and smoke are everywhere, inescapable.

I like getting to rallies early, when things are just beginning to wake up and the crowds are spread thinly on the ground. Down by the entrance a coal lorry was dispensing sacks of fuel to a collection of steamrollers clustered round the tailgate like pigs around a trough. This is one rally

Traction engines on parade at the Cromford steam rally. (Anthony Burton)

where the organisers hand out free coal to the participants – several tons of it – but it is a worthwhile expense for it helps to ensure that they get all the best engines. Steam rallies are not cheap. By the time you have prepared the site, hired the marquees, set up the PA system, doled out the free coal and run up all those small bills that make up a large bill, you find that the expenditure has run into tens of thousands of pounds. After that all you can do is sit back, hope for good weather, pray that no major disasters occur and, with a bit of luck, you may cover your costs and make a profit. So far, they have done pretty well here: 1986 was the sixteenth rally and, as usual, the profits were to go to charity – money going to a variety of causes, from national appeals such as 'Children in Need' to treatment for the dry rot in the parish church roof. Everyone gives their time free and the sense of friendliness pervades everything that happens.

I wandered off for a tour of inspection. There is always a tremendous amount to see on such an occasion and you have to decide whether to dash off to the main attractions or build up towards them gently. Across the parade ring I could see a row of chimneys, each thrusting its dark cloud towards the sky, and the lure proved irresistible. Forty engines were on display, each with its own character and idiosyncrasies. The whole range of steam was there. I left the gaggle of rollers, a dark little group with not much in the way of frippery, and made the acquaintance of an engine which was a complete contrast. *Maid Marian*, a showman's engine of 1926, was built by Fosters of Lincoln, a prolific manufacturer of these ornate creatures. They also have a more sombre achievement to their credit, for they built the very first British tank to join the army in 1915. If you check the smokebox door you can still see a tank emblem, but nothing else suggests the slightest of military connections.

Maid Marian, based need one say in Nottingham, kept herself aloof from the rest of the engines. They stood like guardsmen on parade, and like guardsmen they were determined to look their best when the parade started. You soon realise that a steam engine is very much a family favourite, with parents and children alike washing down paintwork and polishing brass, and what an amazing amount of brass there is on some of these engines. Long before polishing time arrives, however, the mundane, grubbier work will have been done: cleaning out ashpans and grates, and flushing out the boiler, which was a weekly operation when an engine was working full time. There are valves and injectors to be checked, linkages to be oiled. These are all part of the regular maintenance of a steam engine, but behind that usually lies years of hard slog to bring a machine from the scrapyard to the show ring.

Groups tend to form around certain engines. Some go for the massively powerful machines, like a pair of big Fowler ploughing engines – a left-hand engine and a right-hand engine as they are known, depending on which side the cable drum is fixed. There is no attempt at prettification here. They were built for use on the farm, not out on the highway under the public gaze, so there is no need for fancy details and there is not much elegance in their outline. The same could be said of a mobile steam crane, its long neck stretching beyond the line of engines. The steamrollers are necessarily ponderous beasts, but they can shine as brightly as the grandest showman's engine, and the knowledgeable can be found grouped around the oldest engine in the ground. This is a tandem steamroller, probably the last example of its kind. The conventional roller has the typical big, heavy cylinder at the front and a pair of wide wheels behind. But here, as the name suggests, there is a narrow roller fore and aft. It looks odd, but was perfectly suited to its job of rolling down city streets between the tramlines in the years before the First World War. I noticed a well-worn but still legible engraved brass plate on one engine, which gave the driver all the instructions he needed to work the injector. How comforting to know that your instruction manual is bolted in place.

Some distance from the traction engines were the vintage and veteran commercial vehicles and cars, a select group of steamers among them. Sentinels predominated, but a Foden served as a reminder that some steam wagon manufacturers managed to make the transition to diesel. The 1928 Foden in the livery of the Ind Coope Brewery might have looked splendid, but it was not really all that efficient. Where the modern truck has to have a fuel tank, the steam wagon needed a water tank and a coal bunker as well. Consequently, it was heavily laden even before it was loaded with freight. Among the cars, the Stanley Steamer of 1910 looked quite as dashing as any of its more familiar petrol brethren of the period. It is only when you lift the bonnet and see a boiler where you expected to find a piston block that you become conscious of the differences. Looking at this superior little machine, it is not difficult to see why its American manufacturer remained convinced that the future lay in steam, no matter what Herr Daimler and Herr Benz might be saying to the contrary.

As the morning wore on, the whole site became more animated. Music came from different quarters. The sounds tended to merge, and I was reminded of a piece by the American composer Charles Ives, reproducing the sound of two bands converging on one place, but the Ives is more cacophonous than the effect produced at Cromford. Music has always been an important part of the fairground scene. These days the top twenty blare from loudspeakers but, in the days before electrical amplification, mechanical music was provided by elaborately painted and decorated fair-ground and street organs. In essence, the principle is simple: air is blown through pipes as in the conventional organ, but instead of the keys being manipulated by hand, they are worked mechanically through a perforated roll, exactly like that of a pianola. Extra refinement is provided by percussion – snare drum and cymbal – and the brilliant display on the front of the organ often includes animated figures. A frock-coated conductor beats time while a drummer-boy rat-tats away. The sound is unique and instantly recognised by its curious breathy quality, like a tenor trying to sing an aria after running the mile. From one corner of the ground I caught the strains of a Sousa march, and nearer at hand the bouncy tune *42nd Street*. Wherever I went at Cromford, the sound of the fairground organ was never far away.

The fair itself was also coming to life, a mixture of the very old and the comparatively new. There were the sideshows you would find at any modern fair: shooting galleries, bingo stalls, hoopla and the rest. Two attractions, however, dominated the rest. A great, brilliantly coloured conical tower rose up high above everything else, the traditional helter-skelter. You take your mat, climb the stairs and whizz down the wooden spiral to the bottom. This is one of the oldest of fairground attractions and was once known, for obvious reasons, as 'the lighthouse slip'. But the principal attraction was, without a shadow of a doubt, the steam galloper. If you want an image of the old-time funfair, this is it. Some call it a roundabout, in America it is called a carousel, but whatever the name it has been working in funfairs for a hundred years. You clamber on to a brightly painted horse hanging from the circular top on a painted, twisting pole. As the machinery starts up, the top begins to rotate and the horses circle round and round, rising up and down to simulate the action of a galloping horse. It delighted visitors to fairgrounds when it first appeared and delights their grandchildren

The steam gallopers are one of the main attractions of the fun fair at the Cromford rally. (Anthony Burton)

and great-grandchildren today. It always delights me, the pleasure enhanced by the steam engine puffing away in the centre, sending its plume of smoke through a chimney in the middle. It comes, need one add, complete with organ music.

One of the real pleasures of a steam fair lies with what one might call the secondary attractions. There is usually a fine collection of models to be enjoyed, many of them working miniatures. There is the appealing sight of a minute traction engine, large adult precariously balanced on its back, chugging along past a row of its full-sized brethren. Then there are the small stationary engines of all kinds, as loved and cherished by their owners as the mightiest showman's engines. In among these are the stalls selling all kinds of goods, from fish and chips to rally tee-shirts, and a small number of stalls for the steam specialists. Sections of valves, pressure-gauges, machine parts of all kinds are spread out on trestle tables. There is nothing here for the casual buyer, but for some this is the most attractive part of the site. A man swooped down on a table to grab an oblong of steel attached to a pipe which lay among a pile of

similar bits and pieces. He could not have looked more delighted if he had found the Holy Grail. To me it was just a hunk of metal; to him it was the essential part he had been hunting down for months. One stallholder was himself on the hunt for something special. He had just acquired a triple-expansion steam launch engine. Now all he needed was a launch of the right size.

As midday approached, interest centred on the show ring. There are two ways in which you can show off steam engines – the frivolous way and the serious way. The serious way involves setting them to work. The Great Dorset Steam Fair is an outstanding example of a fair where the engines are not seen as mere object to admire.

There are many pleasures to visiting Dorset, including seeing a heavy load being moved by a team of engines, working together, but the one that gave me the greatest satisfaction was watching a showman's engine doing all the jobs it was required to do. The work began with pulling a truck loaded with a dismantled ride to the ground. Once there, a steam-powered derrick was raised at the front of the engine and used to help assemble the ride, in this case the magnificent steam yachts. This ride consisted of a frame with a pair of swing boats, operated by a donkey engine in the middle of the ride. The showman's engine could now take a rest until nightfall, when it took on the last of its tasks. It worked a dynamo that provided the lights for the ride. Stretching from one side of the funfair to the other was a line of traction engines: flywheels turned, engines puffed and the dynamos did their work, bringing the fair to colourful life.

I was lucky enough to make a Channel 4 film about the fair and we were looking for a grand finale for my last piece to camera. To me it was obvious: it had to be on the steam yachts, to round off the story. The only problem seemed to be whether or not the camera could be kept steady enough, but our splendid operator was game for the job. As it would look a bit daft if I sat on my own in the swing boat, we recruited children to take up the spaces: there was no shortage of volunteers for a free ride. Everything seemed set. What could possible go wrong? Well, no one had allowed for the effect of the sheer sweep of the swing, where the boat went from horizontal to near vertical and back the other way at what seemed an incredible speed. I'd often heard the expression 'it takes your breath away,' but this is the first time I'd literally experienced it. All hopes of a steady, reasonable commentary flew out with my breath. It seemed every line was punctuated by gasps and shrieks, and if the message wasn't coherent at least it proved one thing to the viewers: the ride on the steam yacht was a terrific and exciting experience. And at the end that was all that really mattered. This is what Dorset does brilliantly: it shows engines working as they were meant to work.

The other approach is to put them on display to be admired and then show just what fun it is to have a big traction engine. This, to some extent, is the approach at Cromford and many other fairs. The first item on the agenda on the day of my visit was the Ladies' Steering Game, where women are invited to try their hands at guiding a steamroller or traction engine through an obstacle course. It gives the public a chance to join in and discover the complications and difficulties of steering. The easy part lies in being able to see where you are going, for you are perched high on the engine and get a good view of the front wheels. You can then be certain that if they are

A magnificent showman's engine at the Great Dorset Steam Fair. (Anthony Burton)

pointing in the right direction, the whole engine will be going the right way. The hard part lies in getting the wheels to point the right way in the first place.

The steering does not work much like that of a car, rather more like that of a ship. In many old ships, you turn the wheel which then works through a pinion to pull chains attached to the rudder. This is similar, but the chains run down to the front wheels of the traction engine or to either side of the roller. So you have to spin the steering wheel round and round to get any appreciable movement down at the front end of the vehicle. It takes a little practice to get it right, but of course if you have steered a ship you can be sure of having little trouble with a traction

The showman's engines come into their own at night when they serve as generators to provide the power to light up the fair. (Peter Jewell)

engine. Incidentally, please note that steering is not the same as driving; the driver is the one who handles the engine controls.

Other fun and games are laid on for the spectators: a clown does his act, the local junior motor-cycle team perform, but the main attraction is the grand parade. One by one the engines roll into the arena to begin a slow, stately progress; as each one appears the commentator explains its finer points. There is time to give a brief history of each and to point out a few of its special characteristics.

Organisers and rallyers tend to be old friends so there is always a certain amount of banter from the commentator, answered by a toot of the whistle

or whatever manual gestures seem appropriate. Gradually the ring fills with the slow-motion parade and on this occasion, it being high summer, the ring also filled with water as the heavens opened and the rain teemed down. A winching display was scheduled for the afternoon and, judging by the way in which the ground was beginning to churn, it was going to be more than a demonstration. It was going to be a necessity.

Once the parade was complete, and the centre of the ring was full of engines, the crowd were allowed in and, undeterred by the heavy rain, they left the shelter of the beer tent and the open-sided marquee to inspect the engines and talk to their owners. Everyone seemed to be in good spirits in spite of the atrocious weather and it was, like every steam rally I have ever been to, an event character-ised by friendliness and good humour. Drivers cheerfully stood in the rain, chatting about their engines and patiently answering questions put to them. But then you would need to be a patient person to embark on the painstaking task of restoring an engine in the first place. Each engine in the ring was a monument to personal endeavour. No organisation had funded these machines or supplied help towards their restoration. It was all down to the owners, their families and their friends.

As the rally drew to its close, I looked across parked cars and vans to see an immense cloud of grey smoke shooting up. Beneath it was the Cromford Wharf Steam Museum. Here was another of my reasons for selecting the Cromford rally. On my last visit I had called in to see the Wharf Museum, the old terminus of the Cromford Canal, and had then been taken to see the embryo Steam Museum. Outwardly, it was not the most exciting building in the world but

inside was a big vertical boiler, heavily lagged so that it looked like a *yeti* or some other hairy monster. All around it lay a scrapyard of metal which constituted, I was assured, the exhibits for the museum. The assurance was justified, for on my second visit I found that the parts had all been reassembled into working engines. In one corner a steam winch whirred amid a cloud of vapour; a small pumping engine circulated greasy water and a larger engine worked a dynamo which lit up the bulbs on an antique switchboard. Pride of place, however, was held by a two-cylinder horizontal Robey of 1902, its eleven-foot diameter, seven-ton fly wheel spinning busily. This engine had started life as a huge generator, but had more recently been used to power crushing machinery in a brickworks.

There may not be much to the Cromford Canal in terms of length, but no one can deny that it is packed with interest. At the Cromford end there is the Steam Museum and the Wharf Museum; a little way down is the old maintenance workshop of the Cromford and High Peak Railway and the interchange warehouse; and beyond is the Leawood Pumping Station beside an aqueduct – and you can travel along to see the lot by traditional, horsedrawn narrow boat. I cannot think of any other canal that packs so much of interest into such a limited space.

I came away from Cromford, as I always come away from Cromford, with reluctance and a promise to return. It had been a successful rally despite the British summer weather, and Cromford still exerted its old appeal. As I drove south, I caught a glimpse of the Leawood chimney through the trees and looked across at the rain-shrouded hills. For me, steam and the northern moors and mills form a matchless combination – and there was more to come.

Chapter 8

Moorland Journeys

There is a sense of occasion which characterises certain journeys. Steam railway trips inevitably evoke recollections of the past, but my trip by Pullman from London to Yorkshire was something special, full of personal memories.

When I was a student in the Fifties, I took vacation work at Harrogate Station. The *Yorkshire Pullman* was a regular and revered visitor. It seemed, even then, to belong to an older railway tradition, with its distinctive colour scheme and old-fashioned details like the frilly lamps on each table. It was undeniably impressive and I was even more impressed by the magnanimity of the older porter who showed me where to stand to receive the first-class passengers. A woman dismounted, heavily laden. She had something of the looks and a good deal of the demeanour of Dame Edith Evans as Lady Bracknell. I staggered off to the taxi rank, weighed down with luggage, found a cab, settled her in, loaded up the bags and waited. Much fumbling ensued before a sixpenny piece was handed over. Meanwhile, my helpful porter friend was carrying a fraction of the baggage for a jolly woman from third class and receiving four times the tip. It was a useful lesson. As my experienced colleague put it: 'They don't get rich by giving it away.'

I was to have one more memorable encounter with the Pullman. In those days, open carriages were comparatively rare and one became used to hopping into compartment carriages, where the corridor was free of bodies, so that one could hop off again sharply. Pullman coaches tended to get blocked with passengers struggling to stow luggage. On one occasion I took pity on an elderly passenger and agreed to help him stow his bag. The whistle blew, the flag was waved and I was stuck in the middle of a crowd on a train which was rapidly gaining speed. It was something of an embarrassment, but I enjoyed my ride up to Scotland and back.

But now my journey was to begin at the station second only to Paddington in my scale of admirable termini: King's Cross. Its appeal has always lain in its massive simplicity: two great arched canopies forming the train shed, reflected in the twin arches of the facade; but I had forgotten what British Rail architects could do to the splendours of the past. The magic has quite gone, the facade lost behind a vast, new nondescript hall complete with burger bar. The best you can do now is stand – all seats having been removed long since – admire the train-shed canopy and wait for your train. In the best excursion tradition, my train arrived thirty minutes late, delayed by an engine failure which had trapped our Pullman coaches in a siding. However, it was worth waiting for, even if we were to be hauled by diesel on this first part of the journey. It was a Class 47, looking rather smart in its Inter-City livery and, given the nature of my Yorkshire journeyings, bearing a wholly appropriate name: *Brontes of Haworth.*

This is an interesting venture, quite unlike the Red Dragon, and a comparatively new one, still trying to find its place in the market. It started not with a steam locomotive but with a set of old Pullman coaches purchased by SLOA, the perhaps unfortunate acronym for the Steam Locomotive Owners' Association, which can seem phonetically appropriate when a trip is running late.

The Pullman coach originated in America and reached Britain in 1874. It offered a new world of luxury travel. It was better lit, better sprung, better upholstered and roomier than anything else on offer. It looked the part, with its distinctive livery on the outside and attractive marquetry inside. But one important difference between the Pullman and lesser breeds was not immediately obvious: body and underframe were an integral construction using six different woods. The coach looked unusual and remained so, for the Pullman Car Company retained its independence even into the era of nationalisation. Unfortunately, however, when SLOA acquired the coaches they found asbestos linings, fine for insulation but deadly to lungs. The cost of replacement was simply beyond their means.

Then, to the rescue, came Bill McAlpine, who had previously stepped in to save the *Flying Scotsman*. It seemed a good idea to combine prestige locomotives and prestige rolling stock to offer something special in the way of preserved trains. The main revenue was expected to come from charter work: impress your business colleagues, give a treat to the top salesmen, that sort of thing. It worked up to a point, but there were still too many periods of idleness, so Pullman Rail was born, offering – what? Luxury certainly, good food, a steady trundling of the drinks trolley, all things which could be supplied regardless of the train's destination or of what was doing the work at the sharp end. It seemed a good idea to aim for an upmarket tourist trade, drawing in, perhaps, the ubiquitous Americans. Where do Americans want to go? Stratford-upon-Avon seemed a likely venue, and so the Shakespeare was launched. It was unfortunate that it appeared in the year the Americans did not, frightened away by the merest threat of terrorist activity. The Shakespeare was a disaster, but undeterred the company turned its attention to other schemes. Steam and scenery, proven draws for preserved railways, seemed to offer a

better prospect. So it was the Pennine Limited that I joined for my excursion and, judging by the crowds and their enthusiasm, the recipe had worked again.

I shall not dwell on the journey to Leeds, since this is a book about steam, not railways. However, it does have a wonderful beginning, drawing out of King's Cross to give a view over to the spires and pinnacles of St Pancras and the scarcely less ornate gas holders behind it. Then it is a steady alternation of dark and light as a series of tunnels pierces the London suburbs, with occasional exciting views like North London's answer to the Crystal Palace – Alexandra Palace. There is plenty to see on the way, though just what appeals must be a matter of taste. Inevitably, it was the industrial railway scene that attracted my attention: the great brickworks at Fletton, the collieries of the South Yorkshire coalfield, and happy memories of steaming days at Peterborough where, alas, I did not catch a glimpse of anything on the move on the Nene Valley. I did, however, spot a pub sign at Little Bytham. The pub was named *The Mallard*; not after the duck, but to honour the famous locomotive which on 3 July 1938, on the stretch of line just north of the village, achieved what is still the world speed record for steam locomotives, 126 mph. We could not match it, but headed for Leeds where diesel was to give way to steam.

I set out not knowing what locomotives would be used for the journey, so that was the question of the day. Several possibilities existed: *Duchess of Hamilton*, the most powerful steam locomotive, had been used in the past, as had *Sir Nigel Gresley*, close cousin to the record-breaking *Mallard,* and there was a real chance that McAlpine's *Flying Scotsman* would head the Pennine Limited. In the event it was to be none of these, but *City of Wells*, one of that class of lightweight Pacifics designed by O.V.S. Bulleid for Southern Railway. Now this is an interesting locomotive, quite controversial in its day. It is an engine which combines maximum simplicity of outer design, with its slab-sided covers to the boiler earning it the nickname 'spam can', with maximum complication of its working parts. *Aficionados* still argue over its strange, chain-driven valve gear. All good stuff, but as a northerner I felt mild resentment that this most characteristically northern of steam runs should be entrusted to a foreigner from the Deep South.

This is, of course, no more than the expected knee-jerk reaction of northern prejudice and it was such a delight to turn to steam that this minor irritation was soon forgotten. It was to be a memorable run, and not just for its most famous section on the old Settle and Carlisle line. Interest never flags from the moment you leave Leeds Station. As on the *Red Dragon* run down Golden Valley, you find yourself running alongside an older transport route, in this case the Leeds and Liverpool Canal. Railway and waterway climb together up the Aire Valley, through the industrial hinterland of Leeds which they both serve. They go past the ancient foundation of Kirkstall Abbey and a group of sites covering a tremendous range of industrial activity. Two of these drew their power from the river: Armley Mill was one of many woollen mills in the region, while Kirkstall Forge was a major metalworking site. Great chunks of hot metal were pounded into shape, using giant water-powered hammers. A forebear of mine was foreman there before setting off early in the last century for the heart of the Stephensons' railway empire on Teesside. It is odd to look at such a place and muse on the workings of heredity. Was a love of steam transmitted from the remains of these workshops on the banks of the Aire?

Travel this area by road, and it can seem one continuous mass of buildings as Leeds merges with the edges of Bradford. But the narrow valley of the Aire retains its own identity and springs its own

surprises. Coming round the back of Shipley, you steam through the amazing town of Saltaire, with its vast woollen mill built in the style of a Renaissance palace with elephantiasis, its classical church and its neat, suburban villas. It is a town with a history, built at a time when Bradford's mills were surrounded by foul slums. The mayor, Sir Titus Salt, determined on a new type of mill town, one where all things would be handsome – mill, church, houses, public buildings – and where all would be provided for, with library, hospital and almshouses. Only one popular communal building was absent, the pub, for Sir Titus was a sworn enemy of the demon drink. It is all there just as he planned: Sir Titus Salt's town on the banks of the Aire, Saltaire.

All the time, the line is steadily climbing and the Leeds and Liverpool Canal is climbing alongside it, but where the one gains height through steady gradients, the other has to make increasingly large leaps. At Bingley it rises through two interconnected locks, then through three and finally through the majestic Five Rise, and all are on view from the speeding train. The two routes part company for a while, as the canal keeps to the Aire Valley while the railway swoops south to call in at Keighley. We shall be paying a second visit to Keighley quite soon, but now the train rattles through, leaving industry scattered in its wake, as it heads for the town where the two major themes of the Yorkshire journeys unite. Here one finds the woollen mills again, though fewer in number than in the towns to the east, and these are mere latter-day additions to an ancient settlement. Skipton stands at the edge of moorland and fell, a market town for the hill farms, once a fortified centre of power and a turning point. From now on we shall be striking deeper into the Pennine Hills. There is a short pause to gather breath as we collect a fresh crew, and soon the locomotive too will take a breather and refreshment for the second half of the journey.

Long Preston was once a watering stop, not an easy thing to manage these days. Everyone assumed steam had passed away and here we were with a main-line express and a Pacific locomotive requiring replenishment of its boiler. A water tanker was parked on the bridge above Long Preston Station and a hose was dropped down from the roadway. It provided a good opportunity for everyone to mill around the engine, taking photographs of the backs of one another's heads. That water was certainly going to be needed,

for ahead lay the highlight of the trip, the run up the Settle and Carlisle Railway to Appleby-in-Westmoreland. But first, there was a 25-mile stretch of stiff climbing to Ais Gill summit, 1,169 feet above sea level.

The train has a loudspeaker system (sometimes a mixed blessing) and it brought news to delight or dishearten, depending on one's viewpoint. There was to be a delay at Settle Junction where we were to turn north. Because of work on one of the bridges ahead, the line was reduced to single track and, as far as

Probably the most photographed railway viaduct in Britain: a steam excursion at Ribblehead on the Settle & Carlisle. (Anthony Burton)

travellers north were concerned, it was the 'wrong' track in use. Trains heading south normally travel on one set of rails, those heading north on the other, and we were now required to head down the up track. In order to get on to it, we would have to engage in a complex shunting manoeuvre which would be time consuming. Passengers in a hurry were no doubt vexed, but for me it was splendid news. The Settle-Carlisle line climbs steeply away from the junction at a 1-in-100 incline, which is normally taken on the run so that the momentum of the train carries it on its way. We were starting from a more-or-less standstill position so the engine would have to take the full strain, and there are few things the steam fanatic enjoys more than an engine being given a really tough job of work. Up the main line we went, reversed over the points and came round to face the long climb north. *City of Wells* is a quiet engine, but you could hear it now all right.

Last time I had been faced with such a situation was on a steam run to celebrate the Great Western Railway's 150th birthday. We were slowed down on the approach to Dainton Bank and the efforts of two locomotives proved to be of no avail. We ground ignominiously to a halt and had to be rescued by diesel while half the Western Region expresses of the day snorted angrily behind us. There was, shall we say, more than mere academic interest in the climb from Settle Junction. Panting hard but pulling strongly, *City of Wells* charged up the bank in splendid style and headed on for Settle.

There are some parts of the world where responses are so closely tied to one's past experiences that it is impossible even to attempt an objective view. This, for me, is one of those areas. I began walking these hills when I was a schoolboy and my pleasure in them has not diminished with the years; if anything it has been strengthened by the time I have lived away. I was back visiting old friends. This is the land of the three peaks: Ingleborough, Whernside and Pen-y-Ghent. I have walked all three in all weathers and I can look with astonishment at this line, for my mind turns to the men who built it: the navvies living in shanty towns with grand names like Sebastopol, which had little enough grandeur. They fought the moorland bogs, where carts had to be fitted with barrels for wheels to prevent their sinking out of sight. They fought the clay which was so heavy that the effect of pulling a pickaxe out of the ground was as great as driving it in. And they fought the weather, and only those who have known this countryside in winter will understand what that means. They did it, this anonymous army; they blasted, shovelled and hacked through the roughest of Pennine country and the train now follows in their steps.

Having walked this country, I could also feel for the engine and the men on the footplate. It was a fine, sunny day and that for a walker spells effort and sweat. They would be sweating all right up at the front as more and more coal was demanded by the exertions of the panting engine. Between Leeds and Appleby more than four tons had to be shovelled into the jaws of the firebox. And all I had to do was sit at my ease and enjoy the scenery. And what dramatic scenery it is!

This is hill country with everything that this implies. The upland regions remain wild, unfenced, an area where you can walk freely. The peaks rise up to hard edges, the limestone escarpments where weathering has revealed the bare rock. In between are wide expanses of moorland. It is a region where sheep have been grazed as far back as medieval times, and the lower slopes carry the unmistakable signs of the hill farmer. Drystone walls, their light-coloured limestone blocks gleaming in the sunshine, crawl up the hillside to mark off the pastures, and little clusters of farm buildings appear at regular intervals along the way. The fields are still used primarily for animal grazing, so that you see meadows dotted with the soft yellow of buttercups and are spared the lurid brilliance of the rape field which covers so much of the lowland counties. It is land where the underlying nature of the country has dictated man's response. There is an essential unity here. Buildings and field boundaries are of limestone, and that same stone was burned in kilns on the hillside to make lime. It is a country which seems sufficient unto itself. Human activity appears to have made no really strong visual impact. This is not strictly true, but that it appears true, that the overwhelming impression is of wilderness, is a mark of how sympathetically man has worked with the environment. The only structures that impose themselves on the moorland are those of the railway itself.

In such hilly country it was inevitable that major engineering works would be necessary. Hills are pierced by tunnels and by deep cuttings through the rock. Stainforth Cutting, its rocky sides overhung with trees, may look picturesque but on a wet autumn day it can be a driver's nightmare. Even the mighty *Duchess of Hamilton* has been brought to a halt, wheels spinning helplessly on the wet leaves. But the really impressive structures are the viaducts, eleven in all, some small, some big, culminating in the drama of Ribblehead. It was built on a curve with twenty-four arches and it reaches a height of 165 feet above the ground. That alone makes it impressive, but its appeal lies in the wildness of the setting beneath the shadow of Pen-y-Ghent. It took five years to build and a century and more of Pennine weather has taken its toll. The fear was, and still is, that repairs would be so costly that the authorities would decide on closure.

The success of steam excursions has strengthened the arguments for preservation, and there was an encouraging sign in July 1986, when British Rail reintroduced a stopping,

passenger train on the line after an absence of sixteen years. The stops are not without interest. When communities first settled in the Pennines, they did not select a spot conveniently positioned for a railway. Dent Station is the highest main-line station in England, but the village itself is some three miles away. It is, like other stations on the line, a solidly built place, as it would need to be. Stone blocks form the walls, cast-iron frames the windows in small, hexagonal panes. Keeping the weather at bay is a prime concern up here, and you can see stockades of sleepers built around the turntables once used by pilot engines which joined the trains for the climb to the summit, then turned and headed back down to await the next load. After Ais Gill they can relax a little on the footplate, because it is downhill much of the way for the last eighteen miles to Appleby. This is a route that will be popular for as long as rail travel remains. We must all hope that the line stays open – and stays open for steam.

At Appleby we were to turn, say farewell to *City of Wells* and renew our acquaintance with the *Brontes of Haworth* – and you could not ask for a neater link to the next line I was to visit. The Keighley and Worth Valley Railway (KWVR) does indeed run through the Bronte village of Haworth. In fact, there are no shortages of connections between the two trips, for you pass through Keighley on the way from Leeds and the KWVR is also the home base for *City of Wells*.

The Keighley and Worth Valley Railway is unique among standard-gauge lines in that the entire route has been preserved. The railway you travel today is essentially the railway you would have travelled when it opened in 1867. However, the story goes back some way beyond that. The first proposal for a line down the valley intended to link through to Manchester appeared in the 1840s, and among the promoters was the Reverend

Patrick Bronte. It came to nothing and by the time a successful scheme got under way Haworth's most famous inhabitants were dead.

The building of the line was comparatively uneventful, though there was the usual crop of delays, and one unusual excuse. Work could not proceed at one point as no plans were available – they had been eaten by a cow! Two surveyors on the line took time off for lunch and the cow followed their example, munched the plans and did a jig on their theodolite for good measure. Bovine interference apart, all went well and the line settled down to life as a moderately successful branch of the Midland Railway. There followed the familiar pattern of decline, closure and reopening as a preserved railway in 1968. I remember a most enjoyable evening spent celebrating the first fifteen years, when the train ran up and down all evening whilst the ale flowed and fish and chips appeared quite literally by the barrow load. It is a successful line and richly deserves its success.

Haworth is an obvious attraction, a popular tourist spot where visitors exclaim in delight at its steep, cobbled streets. 'How quaint,' they declare, 'how charming, how romantic.' That is the key word, for the Brontes who draw the crowds were surely the most romantic of all romantic novelists. Their influence pervades everything: houses and cafes, gift shops and tea rooms all seem to have decided – each owner having no doubts about claims for originality – to settle on such names as *Heathcliff* and *Wuthering Heights*. Take away the Brontes and you are left with a fairly typical small Pennine town, looking outwards to the moors and inwards to the mills. The great bulk of the

A veteran locomotive on the Keighley & Worth Valley Railway; the former Midland 0-4-0, SF class engine, built in 1920. (Keighley and Worth Valley Railway)

Merrall Spinning Company mill is still the most prominent building in the town. Mill and moor, moor and mill; these are the twin themes that characterise the line, themes which seem to have been with me for much of my life.

To say that the line is much as it was a century ago is no more than the truth. A passenger arriving then on a Saturday morning at Oxenhope would have walked down the cobbled approach road lit by gas lamp and so he would today. He would have found half a dozen trains a day timetabled for Keighley with a journey time of twenty-five minutes. Today's traveller would find seven trains run to a similar timetable, but should not expect to buy a ticket to Keighley for sixpence.

The surroundings have changed little over the years, and as I walked down the line with the controller for the day, I found that I was to be treated to a double-headed ride behind two contrasting vintage locomotives. *Bellerophon* is one of the prides of the Worth Valley collection. Built in 1874 for the Haydock Colliery in Lancashire, this 0-6-0 WT engine continued its important if unglamorous work for nearly a hundred years, having bits and pieces added, subtracted and changed over the years. Having earned retirement, *Bellerophon* sat around rusting for some twenty years before the Vintage Carriage Trust decided the veteran deserved a better fate. Restoration to its original condition was put in hand. The locomotive today is little different from that which left the Haydock Foundry; a simple, old-fashioned working eng-ine, distinguished by a shapely front end where the plating over the smokebox curves down to the outside cylinders. Everything speaks of old locomotive design – the simple Stephenson linkage of the valve gear, the tall shiny dome above the boiler and especially the cab, or rather the lack of it. Victorian footplate men had to be a hardy breed, for they were given little cover from the elements, and

restored *Bellerophon* has only a curved windshield as protection. The footplate looks quite roomy and spectators have a clear view of the few basic controls.

The second locomotive was scarcely less interesting. *Hamburg,* built in 1903, was one of scores of locomotives turned out by Hudswell, Clarke and Company of Leeds for the Manchester Ship Canal. She lost her name in 1914, when anything German was considered unpatriotic, and got it back only recently when she was presented with a steam whistle whose blast had previously echoed around the docks of Hamburg. You can travel behind far grander locomotives on the Worth Valley Railway, but these two small industrial locomotives working in harness seemed perfect for a day on the branch line.

Ours was not the first train of the day. That was a jolly-looking and unusual diesel railbus set, built in West Germany in 1958. There are two of these on the Worth Valley, performing useful work when the service is running with comparatively few passengers. I was to travel in more conventional style on a British Rail standard in the familiar blood and custard livery. There are more exciting coaches in the shed, including a Lancashire and Yorkshire Railway coach of 1878, complete with verandah, once used by company directors. All the rolling stock is notable for being spotlessly clean and superbly maintained, largely thanks to the efforts of a retired policeman who turns up at seven every morning to see to the work.

On a previous visit to the line I had been told the tale of the filming of *Yanks.* Railway sequences were shot on the Worth Valley which, for the purpose, became a Second World War line. Appropriate locomotives and rolling stock were wheeled out, the latter in immaculate condition. The art director approved the choice of rolling stock with one reservation – that it was too clean. So the gleaming coaches were spattered with mud and sprayed with dirty water. It nearly broke the carriage department's collective heart. But they should be used to the ways of film-makers by now as the line has featured many times in movies, and notably in one of the most popular of recent years, *The Railway Children*. Look up the grassy slope above Oxenhope and you can see the house where the film children lived and imagine how they ran down that slope to wave at the passing trains.

Travelling this line, you are presented with a microcosm of West Riding scenery. In the towns, houses huddle and pile up one above the other. They climb the hills in long terraces, punctuated by mill chimneys stabbing up towards the sky. In between, the moorland world appears, where old packhorse routes can be seen wavering off between dark grey stone walls and crossing streams on high arched bridges. Nearing Ingrow, you see something of the traditional life

of the area: allotments and pigeon lofts on one side of the line, the high walls of a mill on the other. Heading towards Keighley, you are entering Lowryland. You pass through a canyon of tall mills built of soot-blackened millstone grit. There is Saturday cricket on a startlingly green patch between the mills. Then you pass at a high level, looking down on a dark Victorian gothic church and more reminders of Keighley's industrial heritage.

Mills suggest gloom, but they are more than balanced by the open stretches of moorland. Stations are built from the dark stone that characterises the whole valley, but they appear as bright splashes in the landscape. Paintwork and flowerbeds go a long way to make these such cheerful places, but, as on the Bluebell Line, much of the colour comes from the brilliant enamel signs. If anything, this is an even more splendid and odd collection – medical preparations guaranteed to

A feature of the KWVR is the varied landscape of splendid scenery punctuated by the mill chimneys rising up as memories of the industrial past: the British Rail 4MT class on duty. (Keighley and Worth Valley Railway)

cure headaches, 'millions sold every year'; Albonoids, 'the best aperient for children'; and products one might have thought of as having a limited appeal, such as Spratt's Parrot Food. Pigeon food I could understand, but I would not have associated Yorkshire with pollies in a cage.

The Worth Valley Railway always seems to be a cheery line, and I do not think this can be entirely explained by the beer sold on the train, good though it is. They have the local Taylor's brew and the fiendish Theakston's Old Peculier. A story goes with that. A party of Americans came by coach to the railway and sampled the Old Peculier. They declared it was just like the root beer they got back home. So one went down, then another and another. They left the train in high good humour. A few days later a letter arrived at the railway from the coach company announcing that there would be no more American visitors, who had learned that Old Peculier was not root beer after all. The coach owners who had to clear up the mess were not amused. The railway officials were.

There always seems to be a place for humour on this line, and a good deal of enthusiasm. I remember seeing a young couple at work on a permanent way gang. I remarked that it was unusual to find wives joining their husbands in shovelling ballast. It turned out to be even more unusual than I suspected: they were actually on their honeymoon. This is a line which inspires affection and I suspect it will not be long before I am back on the Worth Valley again.

My moorland trio was supposed to be completed in style on Britain's longest private railway, the eighteen-mile North Yorkshire Moors line. Once again, it provided the wonderful combination of moorland, steam and a wallow in personal nostalgia, for this was another area where I had spent my holidays as a boy.

I found a line in trouble. A landslip had closed the route between Goathland and Grosmont. Not too much of a disaster, you might think, since it still left a fourteen-mile stretch open from Pickering to Goathland. True, but the loco sheds are at Grosmont and nearly all the engines were stuck on the wrong side of the slip. Only two had escaped. To compound the problems, they were celebrating the 150th anniversary of the railway with a special train for local dignitaries and it was a bank holiday weekend, just when a railway can expect to fill its coffers. The manager could be thankful that one of his locomotives was a powerful 4MT Class No. 80135, a 2-6-4-T more than capable, one would have thought, of coping with the demands of the line. Then its superheater blew. If the fates had really had it in for the North Yorkshire, they would have ensured that the last engine, which would now carry all the traffic, was some little industrial tank engine. They relented.

On loan from the National Railway Museum – on the wrong side of the slip as far as the York authorities were concerned but on the right side for the rest of us – was one of the most powerful and reliable locomotives at work in Britain today. It was a Standard Class 9, a 2-10-0, No. 92220, better known as *Evening Star*, the last steam engine built for British Rail. It was required to work hard all day travelling up and down the line with full eight-coach sets, but there were no complaints from the passengers or the driver. Although there are thirty full-time staff on the line, much of the footplate work goes to volunteers, in this case a man on a busman's or, rather, a railman's holiday; a BR driver from Derby taking a break from diesels and returning to the delights of steam.

Careful readers may have noticed a snippet of information slipped in a previous paragraph: that 1986 marked the 150th anniversary of the line's opening. That places it very much among the country's early routes and, in fact, the engineer responsible for the initial line was George Stephenson. It was planned to run from the coast at Whitby to Pickering. It was not, however, intended for steam locomotives, and horses were to work the line. The profit was to be made from carrying alum from the mines between Whitby and Scarborough, and coal brought into the port by coasters. A few passengers were carried, but in something less than luxury, in a stage coach with flanged wheels which made the long trek strictly under horse power apart from the very steepest sections. Stephenson had opted for a very direct line which meant that trucks had to be hauled by cable up the steep slope on the approach to Goathland.

The line was obsolete almost before it was completed, and it was left to George Hudson, the Railway King, to realise that there was a potential as a route for seaside holidaymakers as well as coal trucks. The line was joined to a network linking both Whitby and Scarborough to York. In time, the old rope-worked incline came to be seen as impossible and a deviation was completed with less severe gradients. This is known today as the North Yorkshire Moors Line, running from Pickering

to Grosmont, where it joins the British Rail system. It is a route with views of a grandeur which can almost match those of the Settle and Carlisle – on a fine day. To add to the gloom caused by the landslip, on the day I travelled England was suffering typical bank holiday weather. Cloud sat on the moorland tops and from the darkness thin, grey curtains of fine rain descended. It says something for the stoicism of the British that they still turned up in force, standing around to inspect and photograph *Evening Star*, myself among them, snapping away with the best.

The line climbs away from Pickering Station and continues to climb for more than twelve miles to its summit among the moors, but at the beginning the locomotive has only the slightest of inclines to cope with, four miles at a modest 1-in-332. How different this is from the return journey from Grosmont where, after a short stretch of 1-in-126, it goes into nearly three miles at a remarkable 1-in-49. As I have said, the one thing guaranteed to stir an enthusiast's blood is the sight and sound of a locomotive at full stretch. Recently, I had been staying in Goathland and heard a distant whistle. I dashed down to the station and above the trees I saw a column of smoke and steam shoot skywards in bursts like an Indian smoke signal, while the blast of the exhaust steam echoed around the hills. There was no need to see the train. You could picture the whole thing; the arrival of the hardworking engine around the bend was merely the completing touch to the scene. This was the part of my current visit I had most keenly anticipated, but I was to be denied it.

There was none of that drama in the start from Pickering. The big engine had a comparatively light load and slid off into the mist with scarcely a whisper, smoke blending and disappearing into the overall greyness of the day. Off we went past the stolid rows of four-square stone houses and the dominating block of the

The last steam locomotive to be built by British Railways *Evening Star* at Pickering station, ready to depart for a journey on the North Yorkshire Moors Railway. (Anthony Burton)

The spectacular setting of the North Yorkshire Moors at Newtondale.

Norman castle on the hill. The rain was no deterrent for the anglers beneath their huge umbrellas, immobile and unmoved by the passing train. I wondered if they were ever tempted to cast a nifty line over to the adjoining trout farm.

A level crossing marks the boundary of the North Yorkshire Moors National Park and the line remains within the park for the rest of the journey. The level crossing also marks the arrival of the woodland which accompanies the route for many miles, some of it mixed with oak and birch to relieve the tedium of the fir plantations. Cross Dale, where a stream in a deep gully defies the efforts of the planters, provides a teasing glimpse of open country. Farwath is a cluster of trackside cottages where the local wood is used to make besoms. The most appealing break in the trees comes at Levisham Station, a charming halt some distance from the . village which is out of sight.

As on the Settle and Carlisle Railway, geography determines where the line must go and it is forced to snake and wriggle along the deep valley cleft, the glacial gorge of Newtondale. The citizens of Levisham have to tramp two miles to catch the train, but at least they find a nice, cosy, welcoming station at the end of the walk. Stone walls and slate roofs are in a style one takes for granted as being typical of this area, and had it not been for the information supplied in the railway guide, I would never have thought of such buildings as being novelties. It was the railway that first brought slate from North Wales and the Lake District. Before that, cottages were all roofed with local pantiles or thatch, as picturesque as anything to be found in Devon or Cornwall. That day, station and station house looked a little dour in the steady drizzle, though their basic attractiveness still showed through. It is the mark of such small country stations that public buildings and private houses are indivisible, with domesticity sounding the dominant note. Take away the platform and the NER clock – still

keeping good time I was pleased to note – and you have just another farmhouse with a well-kept kitchen garden. The cottages by the line certainly look no different. Someone obviously had a friend on the train. A young lady at her kitchen door blew a kiss, but to whom? Close by, a worn sign informs walkers that they should keep to the footpath or risk incurring the wrath of the North Eastern Railway and the ever-vigilant officials.

Beyond Levisham there are more frequent breaks in the trees and the moorland to the east sweeps down steeply to the edge of the line. Elsewhere the thick-set pines are a dark background to the journey, packed so closely that the smoke from the passing engine seems unable to escape but clings to the branches in ghostly wraiths. The tempo begins to change as the climb steepens, a new insistent beat can be heard from the locomotive. One goes on a bit about the noises of steam, but they do have an effect on one's perception of a journey. Just as an insistent beat in music can herald excitement to come, so the changing rhythm of the train can rouse expectations. It does not disappoint. The forest comes to an end and the best of the moorland scenery surrounds the line, stretching out in all directions to horizons ruled straight by rocky outcrops.

Newton Dale signal box is a lonely outpost in this wide land, though on this day the broader vistas were still lost in cloud – including the most famous landmark of the area, the giant 'golf balls' of Fylingdales early warning station. Nearer at hand is Fen Bog, which is exactly what its name suggests; much admired by naturalists for its plants, birds and insects, but roundly condemned by George Stephenson, who had to build a railway across it. Not that this was a new challenge. He had already conquered the famous Chat Moss when building the Liverpool and Manchester Railway and he followed much the same plan here, covering the bog with brushwood and timber until he achieved a solid foundation. It was to prove not quite as solid as it might have been. Some twenty years after the opening, a train with locomotive and carriages was derailed and sank into the bog, almost disappearing. It was not the easiest job in the world to get them out again.

The pounding of the engine eases as it reaches the summit and begins the journey down into Goathland to the accompaniment of a gentle hiss of steam and the occasional grinding of brakes. From here you can see the deviation from the original Stephenson line, which can easily be traced on its way through to Grosmont. Unfortunately our journey was to end at Goathland, though by way of compensation there was time to enjoy the surroundings, for this is one of the most attractive spots in the area and even the foul weather could not destroy its appeal.

The railway company had laid on coaches to take passengers by road to Grosmont. Uphill we went, disappearing into the clouds, and down we came again. Grosmont is the place where different railway worlds meet. You glimpse the original line at Goathland where stone sleeper blocks are on display, with fish-bellied rails spiked in place. Here at Grosmont you can walk along the old line across the Murk Esk through a tunnel, aggrandised by fine castellated portals. The footpath led down to the loco sheds, where the engines were cooped up, unable to move. A short train run down the track took us to the slip and this excursion gave an idea of the world the railways once served. Today, the slip is only a memory and not only has the full service been restored, but it has even been extended, all the way to the coast at Whitby.

Today, we come to this area as tourists drawn by the notion of wild, unspoiled countryside – moorland and dale – but not long ago this was a bustling industrial area. Blast furnaces threw their flames to the sky and molten metal poured out of their bases. All that remains of those days are the cottages where the iron-workers lived. Unmistakably industrial in origin, the cottages are set in close terraces as though there was a shortage of building space in the open moorland. They seem anachronistic, incomprehensible intrusions into a rural world, because all traces of the great ironworks have vanished. The steam train survives, even if it no longer meets the needs of industry; so, too, do a few of those other engines, the great machines that powered the mills and factories of the north.

Chapter 9

Replicas

The building of replicas has sometimes been rather frowned upon as a second-best option. In a way it is, but where originals exist they may be too precious to be put into steam and in the case of many historic engines of great importance, the originals have long since disappeared as scrap. There are several advantages to building replicas, apart from the pleasure of seeing the distant past brought back to

The replica of Trevithick's first road engine of 1801 being put through its paces by members of the Trevithick Society. (Trevithick Society)

life: as Michael Bailey, who oversaw the building of the Stephenson Planet class locomotive that now runs at the Museum of Science and Industry in Manchester, has pointed out, building replicas teaches engineers a great deal about the originals that could never have been discovered simply by reading about them or even by studying original plans.

As explained in the next chapter, my first encounter with replicas came with the reconstruction of the locomotives of the Rainhill trials. These various engines were a prelude to a later set of replicas with which I was even more involved. I had written a biography of Richard Trevithick, the great Cornish engineer who built the very first locomotive to run on rails: though he did not start out with railways in mind. The book was to be published in 2001 to celebrate the bicentenary of the running of his very first locomotive. I was not the only one planning something special for that year. The Trevithick Society was also responsible for building a replica of this pioneering engine.

The story really begins in the eighteenth century, when Trevithick grew up in a family of Cornish mining engineers. His father had worked on improving the oldest type of steam pumping engine, the atmospheric Newcomen engine. That had largely been replaced by the far more efficient Boulton & Watt engine and Cornish engineers were all keen to try their hands at improving on that as well. But James Watt had an all-embracing patent that thwarted them – though young Trevithick tried his hand at a little piracy. One thing Watt was adamant about was that engines should only use steam at low pressure – if you wanted more power you built a bigger engine.

This was fine if your engine was safely rooted to the spot in a solid engine house – not much use if you wanted to move it around. Trevithick recognised that the only answer for portable engines was to use high-pressure steam. His first portable engines could be hauled to where they were needed by a horse, but he soon realised that there was no reason why, if an engine could be used to turn a wheel in a factory, it could not turn a wheel on a carriage and move itself along. So he set out to build a prototype road carriage. This was the engine that stormed up Camborne Hill on Christmas Eve 1801 – and which was to be replicated to celebrate the momentous event.

This was, not surprisingly, a very basic machine. It was fitted with a return-flue boiler with a single cylinder set into it. A crosshead above the piston had connecting rods fastened to each side conveying the drive down to the wheels. This was a system developed from his portable engines, but now he faced a very new problem – steering. It may seem obvious to us, but up to this time if you wanted to move a carriage in one direction rather than another you pulled the appropriate rein, and the horse moved that way, pulling you and your vehicle along behind it. But this was the original horseless carriage. Trevithick's steering system was a tiller to change the direction the wheels were pointing – no easy matter on a heavy steam engine. That was one lesson learned from the replica – tiller steering is hard work. Heaving around the wheels and axle is only part of the problem – keeping the tiller steady to go round a bend is just as difficult. The problem is eased by a simple system of having a board with movable pegs so that once the tiller is in the right position the peg will keep it in place.

Did the original have such a system? That's far from clear. What we do know is that steering did create not so much a difficulty as a disaster. After the first successful run, the engineer set off with friends to show the wondrous machine to the local gentry who had supported his experiments with table-top models. On the way, the engine hit a rut, went out of control and ended up in a ditch. The travelling party decided to leave it where it was while they went off to the local pub. Unfortunately, no one thought to dowse the fire: the boiler burned dry, got red hot and that was it – the whole thing went up in flames. At least the replica is still working and has lasted far more than a few days.

Travelling on it is exciting. This was long before the days of pneumatic tyres and efficient springs, so the engine bounces off every irregularity in the road and as a passenger the best you can do is hold on and hope. But one has to remember, this was a prototype. The main thing was that it worked and Trevithick took out a patent and went on to the next stage – to build a genuine horseless carriage that he planned to demonstrate on the streets of London.

Tom Brogden of Macclesfield built a replica of this, the most extraordinary of all Trevithick's engines, not for a museum nor for any specific event but simply because he wanted to do it, and what a splendid effort it was. The working parts of the original machine were made in Cornwall. Once again, the steam cylinder was set into the boiler, but this time horizontally instead of vertically. The piston rod was forked and the drive went through gears to the crankshaft that turned the rear wheels and to a flywheel. The rear wheels themselves were immense, so as a result the actual passenger carriage sits high in the air. The steering was, again, via a tiller, this time to a single, small front wheel. The carriage had a two-man crew: the driver perched in front of the carriage and the fireman at the back, standing on a small platform to tend the boiler.

The actual carriage that sat above the engine was pretty much a standard stagecoach type of design and was built in London by William Felton of Leather Lane, Clerkenwell. In July 2003, Tom brought the carriage back to London for the unveiling of a plaque on the site of the original Felton works. I was asked to give a short speech and the guest of honour was Frank Trevithick Okuno. The first part of his name explains his presence but the last bit derives not from the great engineer himself, but from his sons, Richard Francis and Francis Henry. They were both engineers and they went to Japan to help set up a railway system and design the first locomotives to be built in that country. They remained over there, married Japanese girls and set up a Japanese branch of the Cornish family. Frank may be several generations removed from the inventor, but he is fiercely proud of his ancestor and has himself a fine collection of Trevithick memorabilia.

It was a lovely occasion and, the official ceremony completed, the London carriage was brought to Regent's Park. Frank and I clambered up into the carriage and off we went, puffing round the park ring road. It's the nearest I'll ever get to feeling like royalty. Everyone stopped to stare, cars came to a halt and Frank and I waved regally to the spectators. Early accounts suggest that travel in the coach was a bit wobbly – a sea captain declared that he was more likely to suffer shipwreck on the carriage than he ever was on board his own vessel and refused to make a second journey. I have to say that our trip was trouble free and very comfortable.

Given the excitement caused by the replica, one would have thought that the appearance of the original on the streets of London would have been widely reported, yet the press of the day seem to have more or less ignored the whole thing. So too did any potential investors: no one wanted to put money into a steam carriage. The problems of steering and rough roads plagued the endeavour and Trevithick reluctantly gave up all ideas of developing a road carriage. Fortunately an alternative appeared that required no steering and guaranteed a less bumpy ride. The road locomotive's days were done: the railway locomotive's days were just about to start.

The next stage of the Trevithick story is not nearly as well documented as the earlier parts, but there is enough evidence to be reasonably certain that the first railway locomotive was ordered for the famous Darby ironworks at Coalbrookdale, near Ironbridge. At any

Trevithick's London steam carriage, built by Tom Brogden, who is seen here in the top hat with Frank Trevithick Okuno, a direct descendant of the engineer. (Anthony Burton)

A replica of Trevithick's 1803 Coalbrookdale engine in steam at the Blists Hill site of the Ironbridge Gorge Museum. (Anthony Burton)

rate, there was quite enough evidence for a replica to be built to run at the Ironbridge Gorge Museum site at Blists Hill.

To describe this as a complicated machine is an understatement. Like the London carriage, the horizontal cylinder is let into the boiler with a crosshead from the piston rod reaching the full width of the engine. Connecting rods move up and down, so that the effect is rather like having two trombone players at work, one on each side of the engine. The actual drive goes through gears to all four wheels, and the whole array is finished off by a giant flywheel. I went up to see it and was invited onto the footplate – not an invitation I was ever going to refuse. Once under way, the gears mesh, the trombones slide and the effect is rather like being the centrepiece of some wild kinetic sculpture. When you've done research on an old engine like this and written about it, to actually experience as close as you can get to the real thing in action is a huge thrill. Then the invitation came that simply woke up the schoolboy in me. Would I like to drive it? I have to confess that all I really did was open and close the regulator but that was enough – and I didn't really trust myself to do the

next bit. It's a short track at Blists Hill and, like the original, the engine has no brakes. If you want to stop, you have to reverse the engine and that's just a bit too tricky for the first time try of an amateur. But I'll never forget the excitement of that day.

The best known of all the Trevithick locomotives is probably the one that ran at Penydarren in South Wales in 1804, simply because it was the first public demonstration of a railway locomotive, and it was widely and well reported. A replica of that engine was actually the first to be built, but in its essential it is so like the Coalbrookdale engine that there is little point in repeating the information. There are two interesting things we know about that engine. The first is that it was not meant to be just a locomotive. It was intended that it should also be used as a stationary engine to power machinery at the Penydarren ironworks. The flywheel on the Coalbrookdale engine would have been useful if the engine stopped at dead centre, but for a stationary engine it would have been essential. The engine succeeded in both its roles, which should have ensured fame and fortune for the ambitious Cornish engineer. Unfortunately, however, it broke the brittle cast-iron rails and was rapidly withdrawn from service. A similar fate befell an engine sent up to Gateshead.

Trevithick was to make one final attempt to persuade the world to invest in his locomotives. He ran a little passenger train round a circular track near the site of the present Euston station in London. It was given the attention-grabbing name *Catch-Me-Who-Can* and although the curious came to gaze and ride behind the little puffing wonder, no one came forward to finance any further developments. A replica of this last engine has also been built but at the time of writing has not yet been put through its paces out on the track. That treat is still to come.

Shortly after the failure of his final London experiment, the engineer was lured away to South America to install his high-pressure pumping engines at a Peruvian silver mine. For a brief moment it seemed his luck had changed – he was paid in bullion and finally had his fortune – for a time. Before he could plan

his return, Simon Bolivar arrived with his army of liberation, took over the country, the silver mine and Trevithick's hoard. Then, to add insult to injury, he recruited Trevithick into his army as the official engineer. For many years Trevithick tried to recoup his losses, ending with running a gold mine. In looking for a route from the mine to the coast and a port for shipment he lost nearly all his equipment and money. He eventually arrived at Cartagena and there the sort of coincidence occurred that if it had been written into a novel, it would have been dismissed as too implausible. Another British engineer was also about to return to England after a spell in South American mines. He was Robert Stephenson – and he had been summoned back to England where he was to be given the task of designing a locomotive for the Rainhill trials. He loaned the Cornishman the fare home and returned to Newcastle to build *Rocket*: which brings this little tale of replicas round in a neat circle.

Completing the set of Trevithick replicas: *Catch-me-who-can*. The original was run on a circular track close to what is now London's Euston Station. (Charles Lamont)

Chapter 10

Steam at t'mill

I did not move on directly from the North Yorkshire Moors to the world of mills, but made a second excursion. In retrospect, that was a mistake. I had been 'thinking North', attuned to the atmosphere of the region, and the spell was broken. Worse, I had to start all over again and travel by car, enduring the tedium of the motorway. We all have stereotypes, one of mine runs like this: south flat, north hilly. I know there are hills in the south and plains in the north, but this is my instant reaction, the response I would give in a word-association test which shows how mad you really are.

My expectations are that as I head north so I shall find the land rising steeply before me. Unfortunately for my preconceptions, my first call on the way north was at Liverpool, where the land seems to get flatter. The visit had nothing to do with my steam hunt, but when you have one subject firmly set in your mind it colours your thinking, which I imagine is the theory behind word association. The theory worked as I approached Merseyside. A signpost announced the turning for Rainhill, and what happy memories that evokes.

In 1979 I spent a great deal of time watching the construction of replicas of three locomotives: *Novelty, Sans Pareil* and *Rocket,* the engines which 150 years before had competed to determine which design would be suitable for the new Liverpool and Manchester Railway. *Rocket,* as we all know, was the winner, and the age of steam locomotion was set firmly on the right track. Hindsight offers innumerable advantages in such matters, but at the time it was by no means clear that Stephenson's design offered the way forward. And when it came to the great celebration, history refused to repeat itself. At the grand cavalcade, *Sans Pareil,* carrying on its shoulders the honour of the Hackworth family and the engineers of Shildon, was the only one to appear under its own steam to start the celebrations. *Novelty* never really worked and *Rocket* was, alas, derailed, although one national newspaper carried a graphic and entirely fictional account of its triumphal progress. The celebrations among the men from Durham went on well into the morning. Those memories of the Liverpool-Manchester Railway were soon reinforced by other names – Edgehill, Olive Mount – and it suddenly seemed that this was an appropriate starting point for an excursion to Lancashire steam.

Down at the maritime museum, you can find a working steam crane and even a steam wagon but, more importantly, you can see the restored vastness of Albert Dock. This was Lancashire's front door: in came the bales of raw cotton from America and out went the finished cloth, distributed through a complex transport network which began with the canals and continued with the railway. Liverpool thrived while Lancashire thrived, and the thread holding all together was cotton, with steam providing power for the mills up to almost the present day. Yet mill machinery was being turned by steam some forty years before Stephenson's *Rocket* sped along the track at Rainhill. Something of that development can be seen in the preserved mill engines, but to make sense of them you need to absorb a little of the atmosphere of the cotton town.

The Lancashire cotton industry was first powered by the water-wheel, but by the end of the eighteenth century steam was becoming important: to power the spinning machines that turned out the thread, and the looms that converted the thread into cloth. The mills clustered around the transport routes which brought them the raw materials of cotton and coal for the boilers, and so the mill towns grew, close-packed and grimy. There was filth and squalor enough in the last century, but a certain grandeur and splendour shone out; nowhere did it shine more brightly than with the engines themselves. But they were seen only by the privileged few. The engine men were kings of their steam castles, undisputed masters of the great machines. Even the mill owners, it was said, asked permission before entering that holy of holies, the engine house. But if there were few who saw the monsters, no one could be unaware of their existence. The tall chimneys rose to dominate each mill town skyline; beneath each chimney was a boiler and each boiler sent steam singing down the pipes to an engine. The pall of smoke hanging over a mill town brought soot and dirt in a steady shower over the houses, but proclaimed that Lancashire was busy at work, providing cotton for the world.

Some years ago I was driving out of Blackburn, which sits in a hollow. This hollow was filled with early morning mist, but as I drove up the hill the car climbed into sunlight and I looked back on an amazing sight. The town was still invisible yet out of the greyness rose dozens of slender chimneys. Sadly, there was no smoke; the age of the great steam mill was long past.

The engines began to disappear in the 1920s with the changeover from steam to electric power; there was also a continuous process of scrapping the old to make way for the new and more powerful. In the 1950s and '60s the steam engines were discarded at an ever-increasing rate, for to the old process of replacement was added a new factor – mill closure.

In 1966, young David Arnfield viewed the disappearance of the mill engines

with dismay. They were a part of Lancashire's history, but it looked as if Lancashire might be left with a few faded photographs and thanks for the memory. Something, he decided, should be done. As a result of a meeting in Heywood, a number of people determined to work to save something from the wreck, and not just photographs and models. They wanted to save whole engines and they planned to keep them in steam, as living witnesses to the past. The group became known as The Northern Mill Engine Society.

The problems involved in restoring a steam locomotive can literally be immense. A massive engine, such as *Evening Star*, complete with tender, weighs in at 142 tons. Mill engines can weigh even more, and, unlike locomotives, they do not come on wheels. When faced with a big mill engine, restorers have two basic choices: restore *in situ* or take the whole thing to pieces and put it together somewhere else. Even that is not simple, because the pieces you end up with can still be large and unmanageable. A 30-foot-diameter flywheel is not the easiest object to transport around the country, or even to get started on its journey. When a big engine was built, the engine house was always an integral part of the design and there was no thought of separating the two. No allowance was made for getting the engine out. Yet here were a few volunteers, with nothing in the way of official backing, trying to shift huge engines which were not intended to be moved. They had to be taken from the building for which they were designed and given a new and appropriate home. The society had to find that appropriate building, and they discovered an invaluable ally.

A Bolton company, Harry Mason and Sons, was sympathetic to the preservation cause. They were owners of the Atlas Mills complex of 1864, which consisted of six separate mills, each with its own power,

Two views of the imposing collection of engines at the Northern Mill Engine Society's museum at its new home in Bolton. (Northern Mill Engine Society)

situated off Chorley Old Road. Spinning had stopped, the magnificent old engines had long gone, but the engine houses remained. Robert Mason offered No. 3 engine house, thus solving one major problem. There was now somewhere to put recovered engines, with a longer-term prospect of turning the building into an exhibition hall. That was back in the '60s, and the first part of the dream has now been realised; the exhibition hall is a reality, and No. 4 engine house has also been passed to the Society. If you want to get some notion of the problems they faced at the beginning and still face today, that is a good place to begin.

Bolton is an ideal place to establish a mill engine collection, for it completes a trilogy of museums which among them tell a good deal of the history of Lancashire cotton. They also represent an amazing contrast in approaches and styles. The Tonge Moor Textile Museum sounds grand, but turns out to be a collection of early machinery housed in a suburban library. Hall i' th' Wood, on the other hand, is a black and white Tudor house which was once the home of Samuel Crompton, inventor of the spinning mule, for many years the most important machine in use in the mills. Such museums take us back to the early days of the industry: they show and explain the machines on which it was based. However, they do not give a sense of the scale of the enterprise, and this is where Atlas Mills comes into its own.

Though Atlas Mills no longer holds spinning machinery, its sheer size makes an immense impression. It is easy to imagine how this group of buildings could contain all the machinery needed to turn the fibre from an American vegetable into yarn, even though the premises have now been parcelled out among a variety of businesses. Here one finds some of the obvious uses for old mills – warehousing, light engineering and so on – and the less obvious, including a sauna. In India, I did once come across a mill which very

closely resembled a sauna. Broach Mill was both old and old-fashioned. The loom shop was huge, dimly lit and hissing with steam piped out to keep the humidity high. With the outside temperature pushing up towards 100°, the effect was devastating. By the time you had walked from one side of the room to the other you felt as if you had sweated off half a stone of fat. Perhaps the Bolton sauna could increase profits by encouraging their patrons to weave while they work. I did not investigate, but made my way to the engine houses.

No. 4 has an air of forlorn dereliction. You clamber up a stepladder to reach the great hall. It is the height which impresses first. Even when one is used to wandering around engine houses, it is easy to forget the scale of things. The big water pumping stations, such as Papplewick, are given a scale by the machinery that fills them. But here the machines have gone and an echoing hall is left, so dimly lit that the roof is scarcely visible in the gloom. Inside is a scrap metal merchant's paradise, an impossible jumble of chunks of iron and steel. Yet cleaned and reassembled this material will become a working engine, a living thing, roused by steam to shake itself back into motion. All that is needed is a good deal of money and a great deal of hard work. Individual pieces weigh tons not pounds and need both technical expertise and muscle power. Stepping carefully between the pieces, recognising a beam there, a section of flywheel here, I thought the task not so much daunting as downright impossible. And this is not a group over-endowed with youthful volunteers: at its heart are men of long memory who recall with pride and pleasure the working days of the mill engines. Is it possible that this small group, working in their spare time, can succeed? Go and see what has been done in No. 3 engine house and you will know that they can.

Again, No. 3 is a great echoing hall, but one which has been restored and prepared as a fitting home for steam engines. There are three principal engines here, each one capable of providing power to drive all the machinery of a moderate-sized mill, but they seem dwarfed by the space. What, you wonder, must the original inhabitant of this house have been like? Well, it stood about 35 feet high, and under the polished floorboards there are some 2,000 tons of concrete that bore its weight. The three engines that steam at Bolton nowadays rest on a good solid support.

This is a steam museum with a specialist appeal; its main attraction is its presentation of a story of technical development and ingenuity. The first engine takes us back to the earliest steam age, when all engines were beam engines. We have met such machines before, but mainly working as they were first designed to work, as powerful pumps. It was not a matter of great difficulty to see that if for a pump rod hung off one end of the beam you substituted a rigid connecting rod and a crank, as the end of the beam went up and down, the crank would go round and round in circles. Thus you would have a turning shaft, and the turning shaft could be used to work machinery; the pumping engine had become a mill engine.

The engine in the museum is of dubious parentage and uncertain vintage, but probably dates from around 1840. Much has happened to it since then. It was always an interesting engine, one of a type very popular in the mills, a double: in effect, two beam engines placed side by side and linked to work together from one source of steam. Two cylinders took low-pressure steam, two pistons bobbed up and down and two beams swayed slowly backwards and forwards. Then it was decided to change from low-pressure steam and insert a high-pressure cylinder for greater efficiency, but it is still a fascinating sight with the two rocking beams working in counterpoint, so that one is up while the other is down and the

flywheel spins merrily in between.

It was soon realised that if you were going to drive a wheel the beam was not really necessary at all; you could attach the connecting rod and crank straight on to the end of the piston, and you could lay the piston horizontally, which saved you the expense of building a tall engine house. A few engineers argued that a horizontal piston would give uneven wear in the cylinder, but that was a false demon. By the mid-nineteenth century there were railway engines puffing all over the country with horizontal cylinders not suffering any harm. So the horizontal engine appeared, and over the years it was to grow to gargantuan proportions.

The Bolton engine, like most mill engines, has a name – *Elsie* – and she is really quite a modest lady, but decidedly up to date and efficient. Built in 1902, this is a compound engine with a 13-inch high-pressure cylinder and a 22-inch low-pressure, arranged in tandem, one behind the other, and with a special point of interest. The mill engine, like all big stationary engines, needs some device to regulate the amount of steam reaching the cylinders so that it can run at a constant speed. One can imagine the chaos on the factory floor if machinery kept speeding up and slowing down in an arbitrary manner. The commonest device used is the governor, which looks like an incomplete pawnbroker's sign and is a prominent feature of many steam engines. The two balls are fastened together and move with the machine. The faster the machine goes, the faster they are spun outwards by centrifugal force, and as they are spring-loaded they partially close the steam valve when going fast and open it when going slow. In this horizontal compound, a different device is used.

It can be confusing at first when you stare at the mixture of rods going to and fro and the spinning discs that make up the steam engine, but it is basically simple – easier to see than to explain. But let us start with a rotating shaft being moved by the steam engine. Now fasten a disc on to that, off centre. What you will see is something which looks as if it is wobbling; it is indeed moving, eccentrically. Anything attached to the eccentric will run out of phase with the shaft so it can make things work in sequence: rods were moved backwards and forwards, for example. They can be used to cover and uncover holes in the cylinder to let steam in and out. In short, they can work valves. When you look at the low-pressure cylinder you see just that, a piece of metal sliding to and fro, directing which way the steam will flow.

On the high-pressure cylinder a different system is at work. The principle is basically the same, but now the valves are spring-loaded so that timing is changed according to the pressure applied and the speed of movement. These Corliss valves do the same job as the regulator – they keep things moving steadily and smoothly. They also click merrily while it works, so that the engine house sounds like a school for Spanish dancers on castanet practice day. You do not have to understand any of this to enjoy watching the engine at work; the smooth interplay of moving parts is always a delight. But knowing what's what doesn't detract from one's pleasure.

What is true of the horizontal engine is even more true of the non-dead-centre engine, a dull name for an enchanting machine. There was a time around about the Sixties when 'kinetic art' was in vogue, when artists produced sculpture which moved in the literal rather than the emotional sense. Its appeal was the graceful interaction of movements. Engineers were not much impressed. They could see that same interplay, that same gracefulness in the practical world, with movement that had the additional virtue of usefulness. I worked in London's Bond Street at that period and would often wander around the galleries, but I can recall no kinetic sculpture as satisfying as a non-dead-centre engine. There is no

photograph of the engine in this book, because its beauty lies in movement, a fluid interplay, all the more impressive for the size and strength of the moving parts. And, for me, there is the extra satisfaction of seeing a machine which is solving an old engineering problem.

In a more conventional engine, you might find that when the whole thing comes to rest, crank and connecting rod and piston are lined up in one straight line. No matter how much steam you try to push into the cylinder, there is no force acting that can cause anything to turn. The motion is on dead centre, and everything has to be moved off dead centre before the engine will work. This is not a problem on a steam locomotive with two cylinders, for the cranks on one side can be set at right angles to those on the other, so that the two can never be in the same position. But what do you do on a stationary engine? Here is one solution: another type of compound engine, but with two cylinders set vertically, side by side at the top of the engine. The ends of the two pistons are attached to two corners of a triangle and the crank is at the third corner. The triangle is set so that no matter where the engine stops, the pistons are never in the same position in the cylinders – non-dead-centre.

To see the three engines at work, each quite different but each designed to perform the same job – to move the machinery of the mill – is a fascinating experience. Yet, looking at the vastness of the engine house, one wonders just how impressive the big engines were. The Northern Mill Engine Society was determined to preserve at least one of the monsters and everything seemed set fair when they reached agreement with Courtaulds that the engine at Dee Mill, at Shaw near Oldham, would be saved. A lot of hard work went into restoration, and eventually the Society was able to hold open days for the general public to see it in steam. These were memorable, but in 1980 the mill was closed and later put up for sale. The new owners wanted land, not a mill, so a final steaming was held. One spectator watched with enthusiasm and expressed his delight, and then turned up the next day to head the demolition gang. Down went the mill and down went the boiler house; only the engine house remained, isolated and lonely. It is still there, officially listed as an ancient monument, but listing means little more than a denial of the right to demolish, not a firm obligation to preserve.

Neglect and vandalism are taking their toll of the great engine. But the good work has proved to be not in vain. The Society had demonstrated that they could take even the biggest of engines and bring it back to life, and soon they were asked to do the same thing again by Wigan Borough Council. Local authorities come in for a lot of criticism and precious little praise. So here is a chance to stand up and call for three hearty cheers for the good men and women of Wigan, and for an act of faith and imagination which has been more than justified.

I went to Wigan by water ten years ago and naturally went to pay my respects to Wigan Pier, still visible as a bump on the towpath. This is what I wrote: 'But the old warehouses that surround the basin are still there, only recently saved from demolition. It is a place full of character, yelling out for new uses that will keep its character intact.' Somebody must have been listening to those yells, for it has come back to life as a major tourist attraction. It used to be a joke calling the platform where coal was tipped into waiting boats on the Leeds and Liverpool Canal, Wigan Pier, because it was just the opposite to the proper piers at Blackpool and Southport. Those were the piers you went to on a jolly day out. Whoever would have believed that the crowds would pour along to Wigan Pier as well. The impossible has indeed happened. The old warehouses have been converted to a lively museum, there are boat trips on the canal, and another of the warehouses has been refurbished as a pub called –

The immensely imposing Trencherfield mill engine in Wigan. (Anthony Burton)

well, I suppose it was inevitable – *The Orwell*. Not least among the attractions is the former Trencherfield Mill and its mill engine. The restoration of that engine was the job the Society took on and triumphantly completed. On 10 April 1984 (very Orwellian) the starting valve was opened and the mill engine turned again.

This engine is a four-cylinder, triple expansion, built by John and Edward Wood. It does the same job as *Elsie* over at Bolton, only on a larger scale. Where *Elsie* produced 180 hp, here we are seeing 2,500 hp. Quite a leap. There are also complications in the working. Steam at 200 psi goes to a high-pressure cylinder, then to an intermediate cylinder and then to two equally sized, and

equally huge, low-pressure cylinders. You can read all the details, but nothing can prepare you for the scale and magnificence of the engines. Yet size in no way diminishes the smoothness of the action. Great cranks swing, valves dip and bob, in a mechanical ballet of perfect synchronisation, in which each moving part cuts its precise path through the air. Make no mistake, this was a working machine, but it is not just latter-day sightseers with strong imaginations who see beauty here. The makers recognised it too. They didn't expect their engine to be on show to thousands of visitors, but the Woods always built in a little extra elegance, if only for their own satisfaction.

The engine *Peace* provides the power for the looms at the Queen Street weaving mill, Bolton. (Anthony Burton)

Some manufacturers enclosed cylinders in square boxes but here they are curved, trimmed and made as fine as engineers could make them. The engine men respected it; paintwork was always kept in beautiful condition, brasses gleamed and the moving metal parts shone through their shield of lubricating oil. In the centre is the giant flywheel, its sides a masterpiece of carpentry, composed of wooden planks which taper from the rim to meet at the shaft. This was the whirling heart of the mill. The rim is grooved to take ropes which loop round and run up to pulleys attached to shafts on every floor. As the flywheel turned, so all the shafts began to turn and set over 80,000 spindles in motion. Now there are only a few ropes and the pulleys turn for display only. Trencherfield's mill engine is perhaps the most impressive sight you can witness in the world of steam, but a vital element is missing. You can sense the power but not see it in use. The engine at Queen Street Mill, Burnley, is a fraction of the size of that at Wigan, but its life and its vitality are real.

Queen Street Mill is a museum, but a working mill as well, and it needs to keep working to survive. The original mill could have been another in the series of casualties in the Lancashire cotton industry in recent years: another set of statistics, a few more on the dole. In its day, it was a remarkably successful enterprise. It was built in 1894 as a workers' co-operative, a weaving mill pure and simple – there was never any spinning here – and it went on doing the same work, powered by steam, using the same methods, and almost made it to its centenary. But decline set in with the 80s' recession and in 1982 everything came to a halt. It suffered in the new climate of modernisation and rationalisation, and ninety-six workers were rationalised out of their jobs. The old-style cotton industry was not merely declining, it was vanishing, and vanishing, it seemed, without leaving a trace. However, there were a few people around who felt that at least the memory of the industry which led the world on the road to mechanisation should be kept alive. The factory age began, for better or worse, with cotton and it deserved something more than an unchecked slide into oblivion. With help from all kinds of bodies, local and national, Queen Street was brought back to life.

The revitalised mill is run with a small grant and much enthusiasm by a new manager, Anna Benson, a textile graduate at Leeds University and self-confessed loom addict. She and her husband collect old looms and store them in a former mill at Helmshore, and she finds it hard to stop adding to the collection. At Queen Street, she has a mill full of older power looms, worked by belt from the overhead line shaft. At the moment she has twenty-four machines at work, will soon add another eight and aims to end up with fifty-six, not working just for show but to produce cloth that can be sold at a profit. This is essential to keep the place alive.

The other element needed is people: not just the weavers to tend the looms, but other skilled workers such as drawers-in and, of course, engineers. Some jobs have gone to employees who were there before closure, but Anna is always on the look-out for new workers. Open days can prove useful. Sometimes she will see a visitor taking a more than casual interest in a loom, and a chat about old working days can lead to the offer of a job. Young people are being recruited, but the pattern of employment has changed. Once mothers recruited daughters, fathers brought in their sons; pride in the mill was an extension of pride in the family. It was a job for life, a skilled job, and if pride had to take the place of decent pay at least the pride was real.

Alan Corbridge, drawer-in, works as nimbly as he did in the past, feeding the delicate threads through the eyes of the heddles, perhaps a thousand of them, to form the warp for one loom. It

A rare sight these days: rows of looms all powered by overhead line shafting and individual belts. (Queen Street Mill)

is repetitive work if plain cloth is being woven, considerably more interesting if a pattern is required. He sees his job as a reliving of a past where work had a strong element of satisfaction, where the person controlled the machine not vice versa. He is not romanticising the past, not saying it was better, simply pointing out that it was different. It is worth noting how times change. In the last century, the steam engine and the power loom had been seen not as part of a proud tradition but as breakers of that tradition, and the opposition had been widespread and often violent.

The sense of personal responsibility is at its strongest in the engine room. Engineers have always been fiercely possessive about their charges and that is true of the incumbent at Queen Street. I do not honestly think he likes the public being allowed to see his engine – it breaks all the old rules. He certainly takes a dim view of anyone else fiddling with it. He

went on holiday recently and when he got back he sensed that something was wrong – nothing he could describe, but just the engine man's sense that all was not as it should be. Eventually, a steam engine troubleshooter had to be called in, but how long will that breed survive? All was in fine fettle by the time I called to pay my respects to *Peace,* as the engine is called. How many engines like this there once were: 500-horse power, tandem compounds capable of driving over a thousand looms. It is almost a midget in comparison with the Wigan engine. But one sees it doing a proper job of work in a working environment. Down in the boiler house, the coal is fed into the big Lancashire boilers to raise the steam which will keep the engine turning over at 68 rpm. This is where you really notice the difference in the working speed, for the display engines simply tick over. This is the real thing.

Out in the weaving shed, the looms clatter; not the deafening noise which

filled the room when hundreds were at work, but noisy enough. I can remember travelling as a boy on buses full of mill girls who would talk to their friends outside. They could all lip read, because that was the only way you could have a conversation in a weaving shed. On my visit, the cast-iron columns of the shed were being decorated with red, white and blue streamers, ready for the official royal opening to signify that Queen Street Mill was back in business. But visitors were already doing the rounds. The young looked around, intrigued by the sight of an old working mill; the old relived their past. An elderly gentleman explained the fine points of a machine to his family; an old lady looked among the rows of seemingly identical looms to find those she had herself worked as a girl. Past and present meet at Queen Street. It does look backwards, but it also has a living to earn in the present. This surely is its special appeal. A conventional

museum can never quite capture reality. Here, you can go down to the shop and do as I did: purchase a Union shirt made of the traditional mixture of cotton and wool, and bearing the proud label 'Steam-woven in England'.

Since writing the original chapter, my wife and I have moved to the old textile town of Stroud, once the centre of the thriving West of England cloth industry. I went to a meeting of the Friends of the Stroud Museum and listened to a talk by Ian Mackintosh about the textile branch of the Friends, who were attempting to preserve and hopefully at some stage run old machinery to keep the memories of this great industry alive. I joined on the spot. Shortly afterwards, the museum moved to new premises in Stratford Park and it was clear that no one was going to be running our old machines, so we formed the Stroudwater Textile Trust. Over the years we've been able to start up two sites, one at Dunkirk Mill, where cloth-finishing machines are run by a water wheel, and a second site at Gigg Mill, where handloom and power loom weaving are demonstrated. There was another site at Chalford, down the valley from Stroud, the beautiful old St Mary's Mill. It's privately owned, but the owner, Audrey Penrose, very kindly allows us to have open days when we can invite visitors to come and see the mill – and among the delights on offer is the old mill engine.

Now I've been describing engines that I've been to see and marvel at, but this was the first time I had the chance to get directly involved in actually doing something myself. There is something wonderfully archaic about even visiting this site. You turn off the main road from Stroud onto a steep little lane that reaches a level crossing. There you have to get out of the car, ring a bell and wait for the signalman to leave his box and open the gates for you. This anachronistic process apparently dates right back to the days when the railway was built, cutting off the mill from the road. To placate the nineteenth-century owners, the lords of the Great Western had to agree to supply a manned crossing – in perpetuity. Is there anywhere else in the country where such a system has survived? If there is, then I've never heard of it.

The mill itself is a fine building of rich Cotswold stone and, once inside, you walk through a room containing an internal waterwheel and into the engine room. And there it is: a Tangye side by side. To some people a steam engine is a steam engine and that's it, but the enthusiast is rather like a wine connoisseur, appreciating subtle differences. Some people's hearts might not beat any faster at the words 'side by side', but to the knowledgeable this makes it a rarity. It is a compound engine in which, not only are the high pressure and low pressure next to each other, but they are both on the same side as the flywheel. The engine is also unusual in

having a condenser – the steam from the low-pressure cylinder is condensed there creating a partial vacuum for extra power.

When I first saw it, it was a handsome engine, but rather badly in need of a clean up: brasses to polish, paintwork to spruce up and most of the oil pots were more or less empty. With a colleague, Keith Browne, I set to work one weekend to oil and clean the engine but not, alas, to bring it back to life. Though the engine had been preserved and well kept, no one had thought to preserve the boiler. We had a steam engine with no steam. Visitors came round, admired it and with two of us shoving round the flywheel by hand, we managed to give them some idea of what it was like in motion. Pistons went in and out, it wheezed asthmatically as the air was pushed around in the cylinders, but no one could pretend that it was altogether satisfactory. What was to be done? There was obviously only one place to go – back up to Bolton. If anyone could solve our problem then the Northern Mill Engine experts were the men to do it. They had moved since my last visit: still in Bolton, but now in bigger premises at a different mill – and with a lot more spectacular engines. I was bowled over on my first visit to the original site, but this was even more jaw dropping. Even if they couldn't help us, it was worth the drive anyway. But, of course, they could. I never really doubted it.

On their grand steaming days, when engines are working all over the museum, their giant industrial boiler comes into use. But sometimes they just want to show off one or two engines, without the expense of raising steam. Tucked away out of sight, there are electric motors driving small wheels, and those wheels run up against the rims of the engines' flywheels. Friction does its job: the flywheel turns and the engine appears to be working. The fact that normally it is the engine that turns the flywheel, not the rotating flywheel driving the engine, makes no difference to the effect.

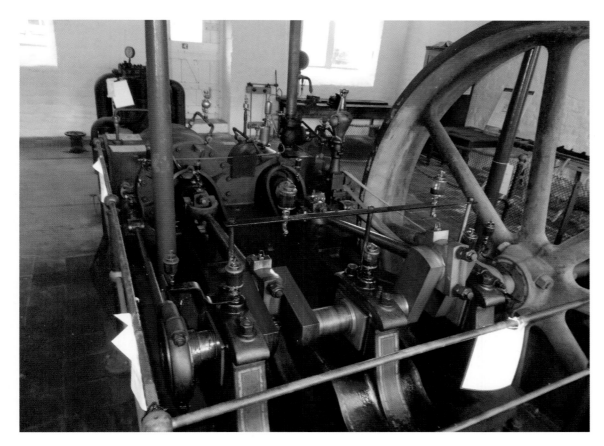

The Tangye engine at St Mary's Mill, Chalford. (Anthony Burton)

Everything moves, pistons go in and out, governors spin and escaping air hisses as loudly as exhausting steam. All that's missing is the smell of hot oil. And what worked for them would work for us. Myself and my two colleagues who were with me were delighted, and one of them, Barry Harrison, set to work designing a suitable arrangement: we even found an old electric motor to use.

Now when visitors come to St Mary's they can watch the Tangye turning over and can admire the intricacy of movement of pistons and valve gear, and without anyone having to do anything much more strenuous than flicking a switch. What we have yet to find is a machine that will polish brasses.

Chapter 11

Hills and Lakes

Sometimes, when I describe yet another excursion to yet another steam railway, a bewildered friend will ask: 'Don't you get bored? Aren't they all the same?' No, they certainly are not. Each line has its own character, compounded of a rich variety of ingredients. Having persuaded the questioner on that point, I am next asked 'Which is your favourite?' I have no answer, because that very multiplicity that makes for variety makes it impossible to make true comparisons. How can you set narrow-gauge Talyllyn against standard-gauge Severn Valley, or compare the rural idylls of the Bluebell with the rougher world of mills and moorland which characterise the Worth Valley? At the more particular level, how can you distinguish between the enjoyment in following a smoothly-working Pacific and a panting Terrier? The task is impossible. Occasionally, however, circumstances conspire to produce an excursion which satisfies every requirement. The next line on the journey north was one which gave equal delight to me and to my wife, Pip, if not for the same reasons. That line was the Lakeside and Haverthwaite.

The Lake District was once a remote, lonely area. Even quite recently accessibility was limited. Then came the M6 and a dual carriageway system leading to the edge of the lakeland of water and hills. Two centuries ago, no one visited the area, then along came the Romantics with Wordsworth at their head and what had been inconvenient lumps of rock became picturesque mountains. The poet who had come to the area for peace and solitude encouraged others to visit, threatening those very aspects of lakeland life he had so valued. Railway entrepreneurs saw that they could cash in on this enthusiasm for mountain scenery to provide revenue over and above that from freight for local industries. Local industries? Oh yes, the Lake District was a busy spot in the last century with extensive iron ore, coal and graphite mines, gunpowder works, foundries, bobbin mills producing wooden bobbins using local timber, and a variety of lesser concerns. With so much going on, there was a good deal of bread-and-butter trade. Tourism would provide the jam.

The Furness Railway struck north from the coastal line linking Lancaster to Furness and headed towards Lake Windermere. There was freight in plenty along the way and the added attraction of the steamers of the Windermere United Steam Yacht Company at the end of the line. Industry and tourism looked like a winning combination, and so it proved until the industry began to fade and the tourists took to the road. But these two apparently irreconcilable facets of life in the area still combine to give a special character to this railway, all that remains of the original line.

You feel the atmosphere straight away, for the car park is the old station yard and you drive in right by the track where, like as not, an industrial tank engine will be getting up steam for a day's work. There is an air of bustle and activity, and inevitable workaday muckiness – you cannot load coal into a tender and keep your hands clean. But that is only one side of the picture. The other is the station and the station buildings. These are homely – not surprising as the stationmaster and his family lived here – and there are pleasing decorative details. The building materials were selected to contrast: a white brick from Leeds for the main structure and banks of purplish brick along the facade with red sandstone blocks at the corners.

The effect is of a prosperous Victorian villa, where you might find a welcome. We certainly did. A fire blazed in the waiting-room though the day scarcely warranted it. This really is a line which makes you believe that you are welcome, a message reinforced when we found the train awaiting its locomotive on the platform. Each carriage table had a pot of fresh daffodils. Welcome to Wordsworth country.

It is not always easy to say why a railway appears to have a definite personality, but here it is derived from two definite personalities, brothers who were actively involved in saving the line and are involved in keeping it running today – Austin and Charles Maher. It began with a love of cine photography allied to a passion for railways, which in 1965 brought them to film the line from Carnforth to Lakeside on Windermere. When they heard of a scheme to take over the Carnforth line to save it from closure, they became enthusiastic supporters. There were the usual fights, one of them with the Lake District Planning Board who wanted to rip up the tracks to create a footpath. That battle was won, but a more powerful opponent appeared on the scene – the County Council, with plans for a major improvement scheme for the A590. The council declared themselves happy to accommodate the railway by building new bridges to cross the tracks, provided the railway enthusiasts paid the bill.

It was to be the end of the Carnforth-Lakeside line. The rail group divided; one set went to work to convert Carnforth into a successful railway museum. The other became the Lakeside and Haverthwaite Railway Company under the chairmanship of Austin Maher, who provided the bulk of the funds. The two brothers, farmer and businessman, had set out for a day's entertainment with a film camera and now found themselves full-time railwaymen. The railway was officially opened by the Right Reverend

Eric Treacy, Bishop of Wakefield. It was among the last official ceremonies he performed on Britain's railways, for in 1978 he died, staying with the railways to the end. He was up at Appleby taking photographs of the Settle and Carlisle, and a plaque there commemorates him with a simple but apt description of the man: 'Railway Photographer, Pastor to Railwaymen, Lover of Life and Railways'.

My first visit to Haverthwaite was to Austin Maher, who had a bad leg which confined him to the office, not the usual way he likes to run the line. Like many another railway, it leans heavily on volunteers, but the brothers are no desk-bound administrators. They turn a hand to anything and everything. There is not much choice when you run a full-time service with a staff of three, helped out by four temps in the summer. It is typical that the man you meet on the platform as porter turns up on the train first as guard, then as ticket collector and possibly as fireman. If anything goes wrong, whoever is on hand deals with it.

Austin Maher told me of the day when one of the volunteer footplate men phoned to report that a falling tree branch had narrowly missed the train as they headed to Lakeside and was now presumably blocking the track. The chairman rolled up his sleeves, collected a bowsaw and went to deal with the obstruction. The branch did indeed block the line, but the fireman had failed to notice one detail: it was still attached to an entire and very large tree. The farmer was summoned but could offer little help. The bowsaw did not meet the need so a chainsaw was sent for and, while the farmer looked on, the tree was dismembered and cleared from the track. At this point, the farmer's sense of ownership reasserted itself and he claimed the firewood. Such is life on a branch line – no pun intended.

Steam was now raised and the train was getting ready for departure. Here I made the acquaintance of brother Charles, on

A former LMS 2-6-4 tank engine at work on the Lakeside & Haverthwaite Railway. (Lakeside and Haverthwaite Railway)

the footplate firing for a driver attired in a greasy cap, less than pristine overalls and, rather unusually, heavy gloves. These, he explained, were to keep his hands clean and soft, a necessity in his professional life as patients do not take kindly to a dentist with oil and dirt ground into his fingertips. He was just one of the regular holiday relief drivers: his holiday, the company's relief. He did not leave a steam widow, because his wife came along as guard and his son cleaned the engines and did other tasks expected of a trainee fireman. The brothers have a decided preference for the amateurs who treat the engines with respect. The BR men tend to give them a bit too much hammer, and paying customers are not over pleased when they have paid for a twenty-minute trip and it is all over in ten.

It was a good morning on the Lakeside and Haverthwaite, journeying up on the 10.40 and back on the 11.10; up again on the 11.40 and back again on the 12.15. The first journey was in the conventional carriage with its welcoming daffodils, and this short line certainly crams in plenty of interest. What a lot of changes this little section of railway has seen. The nature of the landscape might not be obvious to the casual observer, who sees pleasant scenery with a busy river bustling down to swell the waters of Lake Windermere. But you do not have to look very closely to see that the area's past was far removed from the popular tourist image of lakeland. Almost as soon as you leave the station, you see what appears to be a double-track line, but which soon reveals itself to be a single line and a head shunt, the latter leading off towards crumbling industrial remains. This was once the Backbarrow Ironworks, where iron was made for close on 300 years. Technologies changed but the works went on, and for its last half century the iron ore came down the railway to be unloaded for the furnaces.

Backbarrow is, at first sight, a typical lakeland village of stone houses, roofed with slate. Passengers often exclaim over the picturesque falls on the River Leven; this is no natural waterfall but a weir, built to supply power to the local cotton mill. It was once a scene of degradation as complete as one could find in the worst industrial slum in Lancashire, with mill children crammed into the apprentice house under conditions which would be considered appalling in the most rigorous borstal, while families were scarcely less cramped in the village itself. The misery has ended but the buildings survive.

The village is attractive now that these evils have been removed. Even the mill has undergone a series of metamorphoses. Cotton spinning has long ended, but until recently it was used as a factory for making ultramarine. Now that has finished, the industrial life has disappeared and it has been turned into a hotel. It says something for the quality of the building that it can come to terms with such a variety of uses. Its appearance had changed considerably since my previous visit, when it was still at work and everything around it was stained a vivid blue. In my notes of that visit I jotted down: are laundries still using the old blue bags? The answer is now clear: no, hence the hotel. Occasionally, as I travel around the country, I have the blasphemous thought that we might all be better off if we began turning tourist hotels into factories. It would work rather well as the elegant mills of the eighteenth century would provide attractive accommodation, and the square-block hotels of our age would serve very nicely as factories.

Beyond the mill hotel, the river calms down and romantic scenery takes over from the industrial landscape. Lake steamers used to come up the river to the Swan Hotel at Newby Halt, a hotel with a long history of serving lakeland visitors as a coaching inn, then as a staging post between railway and steamboat. It represents the new lakeland that began to take over more than a century ago, and now the process is complete. The industrial worker's cottage is a holiday home and the dour Methodist chapel is one of the few reminders that the area was one of settled communities, not transient visitors.

The lake has long been a favoured spot for the pleasure seekers, as some grand boathouses testify. The railway brought more trade to the busy lake steamers, a role it still fulfils, even if the steamers no longer steam but are dieselised. Outwardly the vessels have not changed much and the fleet still includes the extraordinary *Tern,* built in 1891 and looking like an overgrown Canadian canoe, with its sweeping, upcurved bow. But just as *Tern* has lost the magic of steam, so the station has lost its grandeur. Its splendid Italianate towers have gone. At one time it looked as if it had been picked from the shores of Lake Como and dropped beside Windermere, but now the buildings are sadly commonplace. Only the lake remains unchanged, with its long vistas of the distant hills. The lake was, indeed, to provide the setting for the next stage of the journey, across to the town of Windermere for a powerful dose of nostalgia. But I was not yet ready for that. First I went back to Haverthwaite and then repeated the entire journey from a different viewpoint.

I have never turned down an opportunity to ride on the footplate, and on two lakeland journeys I experienced such contrasting rides that I decided to share them with the reader.

Back at Haverthwaite, I changed from a carriage to the cab of *David,* a typical industrial tank engine used for heading light, off-peak services. It is an appropriate engine to find on this line for its working days were spent at Millom Ironworks, shunting pig iron and coke between rail terminal and works. It was a busy little engine and it certainly has to work hard here. This may be a short line, but it is a demanding one, both for the engine and for the men in charge.

Starting a steam engine from rest and getting it under way is both like and unlike driving a car. You do not start a car by putting it straight into top gear, nor do you a steam locomotive. A learner driver soon discovers that a hill start is more difficult than a start on the flat; a lesson soon learned by the locomotive driver as well. There, however, similarities end. It is possible to draw analogies between regulator and accelerator, between reverser and gear change, but they are false. To understand the complications of the start, you have to have appreciation of the controls. Here is a simplified version.

The fireman's job is to provide enough heat in the firebox and water in the boiler to ensure that the driver has sufficient steam available at the right pressure whatever the demands on his engine. This is not just a matter of throwing a lot of coal on the fire. The coal has to be added at the right time and to the right part of the grate to ensure regular, even burning and a constant watch must be kept on the water gauge to see when more water needs to be added to the boiler. The water is passed from the tank to the boiler by the steam injector, which forces the water down the pipes on a jet of steam. It is all a matter of judgement, experience and damned hard work.

The driver has three primary controls: the brake, the regulator and the reverser. The brake needs no explanation. The regulator does what its name implies, regulates the amount of steam passing from the boiler to the pistons. The reverser is more complex. Obviously, you need to be able to run the locomotive backwards and forwards, and at its simplest this is what the mechanism does: a device – in our engine a lever – can switch the direction of the engine's movement. Full forward, it runs forward; full reverse, backwards. However, there are positions in between which affect the movement of the valves. In full forward, or full reverse, the valves are opened wide to allow the maximum amount of steam into the cylinder, giving maximum impulse to the piston to overcome the inertia of the great, lumbering chunk of iron and steel that is a steam locomotive. Once the engine is moving, you need to cut the steam off sooner to allow it to expand in the cylinder for free, swift running. Nowhere can you find a better example of the complexities of this process, of the need for good judgement, than at the start of this line.

I joined the engine as we ran back up into the tunnel through the rock that marks the end of the line at Haverthwaite. Points were switched and we ran forward and then back again to link on to our train. The clock ticked over to start time, the whistle blew and the guard gave 'right away'. Brakes were released and it was time to move. The reverser was pushed full forward and the driver began his hill start up a fierce l-in-70 gradient. You have to learn to 'feel' the regulator, easing it just the right amount to prevent embarrassing spinning of the wheels. Steam blasted into the pistons and out of the exhaust. As it passed up the chimney, the exhaust steam sucked at the flues of the firebox and tore at the fire and the fireman had to swing his shovel to repair the damage – coal at the back, shot off the end of the shovel, coal at the front and coal at the sides, all to be shaken by the engine movement towards the centre to produce an even fire. As the engine gained momentum, the reverser was pulled halfway back towards the mid-position and the regulator brought to fully open. The train shot into the tunnel ahead with steam and smoke billowing down from the rock roof around the cab.

We were on our way, but there was no time to relax for we immediately reached a sharp bend, the wheel flanges singing on the metal. To this cacophony was added the whoosh of the injector as water was fed along to replace the vast quantities we had converted to steam in such a short time. Only then could everyone say that the journey had safely begun.

After that, life was relatively calm, keeping things going to the summit and then a gentle glide down to Lakeside. There was one stop along the way and signals to watch out for – the sort of thing which delights the railway buff because the old semaphore signals are still on lattice towers, in a style characteristic of the old Furness Railway. There was plenty to do, with all the safety regulations that go with single-track running, but the real excitement was in those first hectic moments. No two drivers will tackle the line in the same way, just as no two engines will perform identically. It is in the difference that the fun lies, which is where we began this account of a day on the Lakeside and Haverthwaite Railway.

After all that excitement, something calmer seemed appropriate: calmer but not less interesting. Railway passengers often used to continue their journey by well-appointed lake steamer. Cargo was sent by the railway company's own steam cargo boat, the SS *Raven*, built at Rutherglen on Clydeside in 1871, a sturdy, practical vessel with no claims to elegance. A small hand crane was mounted on the deck and her powerful bows were often used as icebreakers to clear the way for the passenger boats in winter. Her working life may be over, but she is far from finished. The honest, hardworking old lady is taking her ease in polite society, surrounded by some of the most beautiful boats ever built, the steam launches of Windermere.

I first came to the Windermere Steamboat Museum in 1979, and met its founding father, George Pattinson. I was enchanted, and was able to go back later to film three of the vessels on the water for the televison series *The Past Afloat*. Whenever I return I am equally delighted and there always seems to be something new and exciting added to the collection. But before visiting newcomers, one should pay one's respects to old friends and should certainly start with the eldest.

The end of the line beside Lake Windermere with the 1938 MV *Swan* out on the water. (Lakeside and Haverthwaite Railway)

Dolly is not only the oldest vessel in the collection, she is the oldest mechanically powered boat anywhere in the world. She was built in 1850, when Windermere was just beginning to take on its present character. In 1847, the Kendal and Windermere Railway, a branch off the Lancaster and Carlisle, reached the hamlet of Birthwaite. The prosperous mill owners of Lancashire fancied the idea of leaving the smoky towns where their fortunes were being made to spend the summer in country houses down by the lake, in the comfortable knowledge that the train was available to take them back to the mill. Birthwaite blossomed, and with growth there came a new name, Windermere; and out from the boat houses at the water's edge puttered the first steam launches, *Dolly* among them. Old age eventually overcame them and would no doubt have overcome *Dolly* but for a fortuitous event. It is an old story but still worth the telling.

Dolly was already past her prime when she was bought and taken to Ullswater, where she lay at her moorings in the severe winter of 1894. The ice gathered the old launch in its grip, the planks opened and down she went, fifty feet to the bottom of the lake. Had she not sunk, deterioration would certainly have taken its toll, but a peaceful rest on the lake floor in non-corrosive water did little harm. The great age of the steam launch passed and the vessels became rarities, so when a local diving club found her by accident on a routine dive in 1960 there was tremendous interest. It was decided to raise her – neither an easy nor a quick process, but in November 1962 *Dolly* was floating again and the long task of restoration began. It was extraordinary how much had survived: not even new piston rings were needed. *Dolly* came back to Windermere, not as an object in a museum case but as a working machine which can and does steam out on to the waters her fine clipper bows first saw in 1850.

Historically, *Dolly* is the outstanding vessel in the collection, but for many who come here the appeal is in the boats, not as examples of marine technology but as evocative survivors from the end of the Victorian age. They call forth images of Victorian and Edwardian England: of summer idylls on a placid lake beneath an unspoiled blue sky; of men in blazers and women in muslin; of picnics on islands and a sense of unchanging calm. There is no point in saying that it must have rained sometimes, or that this was an idyll enjoyed by only a privileged few. The boats will have nothing to do with such cavilling, for the beauty of their lines and the superb quality of materials used combine to suggest something akin to perfection. No wonder someone like George Pattinson could not bear to see them disappear. He has known the launches since his childhood, when the family would go out on the lake with just enough firewood to get them to the island where the children would collect supplies for the return. To walk around the boat-house where the launches bob quietly by the landing stages is to see more beauty in one spot than is possible anywhere else in the country. But the real treat came when we took to the water.

George Pattinson introduced us to the latest acquisition: *Kittiwake,* a vessel with a history almost as romantic as *Dolly.* She was built in 1898, a slim, sleek vessel, 40 feet long but only 7 feet in the beam. With her straight bows and pronounced counter at the stern, the whole constructed in a rich, dark teak, one could not ask for a smarter hull. Above that there is a little aft day cabin, glass-sided and upholstered in green velvet, where the family could sit in some splendour. Hardier members could take the air out at the stern. Like a Victorian train, there was a strict class division between the aft end of the boat – family – and the front part, given over to engine and boatman. The Victorian family launch was not like the modern motor launch. It was not expected that anyone in the family would know how to work the engine, nor would they think it proper to do so. That was the engine man's job,

and in the museum you can see pictures of some splendid boatmen, some wearing jerseys carrying the name of the launch they served. I like to think that some owners shared George Pattinson's love for the whole vessel and showed equal enthusiasm for the working parts.

That, then, is the *Kittiwake:* very much a Windermere boat, built in Bowness and owned by the Groves family of Holehird House until 1939. After the war it changed hands, and more importantly changed engines, steam giving way to petrol. George Pattinson asked what had happened to the old engine. It had been sold. He jotted down the address of the new owner on the back of a cigarette packet. Years later, *Kittiwake's* last owners, Mr and Mrs Brownson of Windermere, generously donated the launch to the museum, and the hunt was then on for the missing engine. All George Pattinson had to do was to remember where he had left the cigarette packet twenty years before. Astonishingly, he found he still had it, providing the clue which led to its being traced to the Penrhyn Castle Museum in Wales in 1983. The curator lent it to Windermere, and it is now back in the launch.

When the launch was built, she was fitted with a compound engine by Sissons, the well-known manufacturers of small

The steam launch *Dolly*, built in 1850, is thought to be the oldest surviving mechanically driven vessel still afloat in the world, seen here on Lake Windermere. (Windermere Jetty Museum)

The Windermere Steam Boat Museum has a magnificent collection of elegant launches. Here are just two of them, *Osprey* and *Kittiwake*. (Windermere Jetty Museum)

marine engines. That first engine came out after three years to be replaced by the present beauty – a triple-expansion engine from the same manufacturers. Three tiny cylinders, 5 inches, 6¼ inches and 8 inches, are to be seen side by side, each with a piston and connecting rod leading down to cranks on the propeller shaft. It looks like a toy, but the three cylinders provide more than sufficient power to keep the 9-ton vessel moving with effortless ease through the water. We started from cold, but in no time a few barrow loads of logs were on board, the fire was lit in the boiler and the pressure gauge was climbing. We were off. The first thing that strikes you is the almost perfect silence; there is a distant gurgle from the propeller, the faint hiss of steam and a mere whisper from piston and crank. The next thing you notice is the odd steering position. I am used to boats where you stand or sit facing the bows with the wheel in front of you. Here, however, as the boatman had to be both engineer and helmsman, the wheel is set to one side and at right angles to the direction of travel. So you turn the wheel towards the bows if you want to go to port, to the stern for starboard. A more conventionally positioned wheel was also supplied in case any of the family wanted to take over the steering. Of course, they did not need to worry about the engine or feeding the boiler with logs.

There is no denying it, being on the lake in a steam launch gives one a feeling of immense superiority. You are smug in the knowledge that nothing else is going to be as fine as *Kittiwake.* Johnny-come-lately motor launches dash noisily about the place, but their noise and speed excite no envy. One could, in any case, match them for speed – without the noise – by bringing out the steam speed launch *Otto,* capable of eighteen miles per hour. But the Windermere launch was not built to rush around in an unladylike fashion. It was designed for a tranquil passage which not only leaves the occupants undisturbed, but leaves the wild life and other lake users undisturbed as well. An excursion steamer went by and every head and camera turned our way. We smiled and waved nonchalantly, conscious of how fine a picture the launch made, gliding through the light-spangled wash of the cruise ship. The only other vessel I could be in on that huge lake and feel no sense of inferiority to the steam launch would be one of the few remaining Windermere yachts.

Anyone who has known Windermere only from the land, driving down twisting lakeside roads or fighting through the holiday crowds in the town centre, can have no concept of how different things are from a steam launch. The water changes continuously with the shifting light; the sun glitters on the wavelets; wooded hills swoop down to the water's edge; tree-covered islands dot the lake, and the Langdale Pikes rise darkly above the horizon. These hills often seem unreal, like the cardboard cut-out mountains of a toy theatre, so hard and precise is their silhouette. It is said there was a time when every local family who could afford it owned a steam launch. I am not surprised. If there is a better way to enjoy the lake, I do not know it. However, the mountains and the lakeland fells remain remote and distant. To reach the heart of the hills by steam you must leave the water and return to the land.

From Windermere I drove towards the west coast on one of the most exciting roads in Britain. The road across Hardknott Pass rises to 1,300 feet, snaking up steep gradients in a series of hairpin bends. What wonderfully clever men modern road engineers are, you think to yourself, then you reach the top and find a Roman fort and a Roman road. From the top of the pass you look down into Eskdale and you ponder the daunting task facing the men from Italy: road construction in this darkly inhospitable northern land. Great romantic revivals seem to permeate the air of the Lake District, and the Ravenglass and Eskdale Light Railway has a history full of romance and one which raises the pulse rate of all railway enthusiasts of, shall we say, a certain age. The beginning of the story could scarcely be more prosaic, for it was just one of many industrial narrow-gauge railways, built on this occasion to bring iron ore from the mines of Eskdale to the coast at Ravenglass. Trade declined, closure followed and that should have been the end of the story. But up stepped the schoolboy's hero, Mr W.J. Bassett-Lowke, builder of model trains. How many stared wide-eyed at his model engines and carriages, built to a standard unattainable by the mass manufacturers of model railways? For most of us, they represented an impossible dream, but Bassett-Lowke had dreams of his own, of miniature locomotives working a proper passenger railway. He saw the Ravenglass to Eskdale goods line as a potential tourist route, linking seaside to hills. He also saw it as the ideal testing ground for a 15-inch-gauge railway. He devised the tourist route, but new quarries at Beckfoot provided the diminutive railway with welcome freight traffic as well. The quarries proved to be major money earners and their closure in 1953 threatened the existence of the line. But by then the Ravenglass and Eskdale or, to give it its more homely nickname, the Ratty, was established in the public affection. A trust was set up to run the line and still runs it today.

The pleasures of the Ratty are what they have always been. In part they derive from the scenery, but no less important is the delight of a world in miniature. The model railway on the bedroom floor has grown and grown to the point where the child no longer has to be content with looking at and manipulating the controls from outside the rail system. He or she can clamber into the little railway and become part of it. The Bassett-Lowke engine has gone from the shop window,

its glass smudged by countless numbers of snotty noses, and has come out ready to tackle a real job of work.

This western fringe of lakeland has less popular appeal than Windermere, not because it is less attractive but because it is farther from the motorway, which adds to its appeal for some. The Ratty takes you through some superb scenery and I was faced with that familiar conflict of interest, between the delights of the landscape and the pleasures of the footplate. I had not the least hesitation in accepting a footplate ride, for the traveller on the miniature engine has a better view than the passengers travelling in the coaches behind.

The locomotives on the Ratty are quarter scale, which is not an easy thing to envisage, but if you think of a main line express designed for a crew about eighteen inches tall you might get the idea. Obviously, a full-sized adult is not going to be able to stroll around the footplate of a Ratty locomotive, so instead the driver sits, looking out over the top of the boiler, feeding pieces of coal with a tiny shovel into a small firebox while handling the scaled-down controls. But these are no toys, no fairground fun rides. The locomotive I travelled on was *River Mite*, specially built for the line in 1966. It is a 2-8-2 and if this were a standard-gauge engine you would be expecting power and speed. This is what you get, scaled down; this engine does real hard work. In 1985 it covered 4,215 miles and hauled 100,000 passengers over the seven-mile route where gradients rise to 1 in 40. The run takes approximately forty minutes, which may not sound much, but scale it up and you have a heavy train working at an average speed of 42 mph over a tough, uphill route. Not many engines could match that performance.

There can be no better introduction to the working of a steam locomotive than a ride alongside a driver on the Ratty, especially when the controls are in the hands of Ron Clarke, an experienced ex-British Rail

driver. It was a supreme example of a man in tune with a machine, controlling it by deft touches, everything being done to a well-understood pattern but responsive to those small changes which ensure no two days on the footplate are ever the same. Ron 'played' his locomotive as a *maestro* might play a musical instrument. Here he would provide a delicate touch on the regulator, there he would move the reverser a notch forward or back. Being both driver and fireman meant paying equal attention to both roles. With steam pressure rising, there was a risk of blowing off, excess steam whistling uselessly out into the air, so he reduced the heat of the fire. He picked a suitable piece of coal from the tender and propped the firebox door open just enough to cool things down. Alternatively, he could turn the injector on and provide some extra water for the fire to heat.

Water levels and steam levels are constantly checked, but the real secret of economical running lies in knowing the road. This means that you know when to take a run at a gradient, and when you can relax and coast comfortably along; when you can slow down, or when you need to quicken the tempo. The driver who ends his run with every stop met on schedule and minimum fuel used has achieved all that anyone can expect of him. He is not likely to be given any medals, but he will know that he has used all his skills to achieve a good day's work. But even the best drivers may falter when faced with the unexpected.

In spring on the Ratty, lambs are a perpetual hazard, but they can usually be sent bounding off into the bracken by a sharp blast of the whistle. Ron told me that just before our run he had been brought to a stop by a lamb, minutes

The 2-8-2 locomotive *River Mite*, based on an original LNER design of the 1930s by Sir Nigel Gresley, on the Ravenglass & Eskdale Railway. (Ravenglass & Eskdale Railway)

rather than hours old and too weak to get out of the way. He had to pick it up and move it to one side, but the wretched beast had elected to get itself born halfway up one of the steepest inclines. Restarting was no easy matter. Animal life of all kinds abounded along the route: a deer strolled nonchalantly across the tracks to disappear into the woods; rabbits hopped everywhere; a profusion of bright jays whirred and a buzzard circled above the hill.

With so much happening it is easy to forget the superb views on all sides. This is lakeland scenery at its best. The world was that of moorland and woodland; of fern-covered slopes through which the granite crags erupt; the jagged rocks hard-edged, contrasting with the soft movement of the bracken. There were signs of human activity too: in Muncaster Watermill, now restored to working order; in the disused quarries; and in the hill farms which seem to have grown up with the land. All the time, as you climb, the hills get closer, dominated by Scafell, England's second highest mountain at 3,162 feet, just masking the sister peak 48 feet higher, Scafell Pike.

This railway has something for everyone, and I did not feel embarrassed as I had on Snowdon, travelling by steam instead of on foot. The Ratty takes in all aspects of the region, not just the romantic land of Wordsworth and the wild country beloved of walkers and climbers, though the latter are well catered for. You can choose from a selection of 'Ratty Walks' devised by the great Wainwright himself, but as befits a former working railway, you also get a glimpse of the human history of the region.

The Lakes have seen industry come and go, from the days of the 'axe factory' of Langdale when neolithic man worked to shape the local stones, to the nuclear power station which dominates the shoreline north of Ravenglass. In between come the remains of the mines and quarries which first called the little line into being. The totality is something more than the sum of the parts, but the most lasting impression was of seeing a craftsman demonstrating his skills. On my next journey, I was to give up my passive role as spectator and take an active part in the world of steam.

Chapter 12

Bucket and Spade

Nowadays you have to be of a certain age to have memories of the thrills of going by train for a seaside holiday in the days of working steam. There was something about waiting at the station, looking out for the distant cloud of smoke and listening for the blast of a whistle, which added to the air of excitement. Then the panting beast would finally appear, there would be a squeal of brakes and you'd find a compartment and, if you were lucky, a seat by the window. Then you were off and every stop along the way seemed specially designed to frustrate you, when all you wanted was to get that first glimpse of sea and sand. Our family were not great ones for seaside holidays – or any other kind come to that – but I did have an aunt and uncle in Morecambe and we would stay with them. We always went by train and I still have vivid memories of those journeys, not all of them happy ones. I recall one trip where we shared our compartment – a fact that alone says how long ago this was – with a family who had a young daughter who kept up a chant for, it seemed to me, the entire journey. 'Morecambe, Morecambe come to me. I love you and you love me.' Being a pedantic child I would have liked to point out that it wasn't coming to her she was going to it, and I had an even stronger desire to find a way of gagging her. But mostly the memories are of that growing excitement of waiting to arrive, the sense of anticipation so great that the reality when we got there would never quite live up to the thrill of the journey.

We can never quite recreate that world of childish wonder, but a trip to the seaside by steam train still evokes special memories that no other rail journey can manage. My exercise in seaside nostalgia took place on a sunny day in May on the West Somerset Railway, which lays claim to be the longest continuous preserved line in Britain. Historically, however, it is not quite continuous. It began life as the West Somerset Railway, running from the Bristol & Exeter main line at Norton Fitzwarren to what was then the busy little harbour at Watchet. It was not a very propitious beginning: authorised in 1857, work only began two years later and the line wasn't finally opened until 1862. This was seen largely as a goods line, but when Victorians started showing a passion for seaside holidays, plans were laid for developing the little harbour at Minehead into a major resort – and there was only one way that could happen: it would have to have a railway. The extension was nominally an independent Minehead Railway, approved in 1865, but investors seemed reluctant to put up any money, so the company was dissolved in 1870, reformed a year later and work began. Enthusiasm was not very much greater than it had been before, and the company was constantly running out of funds. At one point things got so bad that the navvies weren't paid and they tried to storm the clerk of works office and had to be held back at pistol point. It was finally opened in 1874 and became part of the broad gauge system of the West Country, eventually being absorbed into the Great Western empire.

In spite of the dithering over raising finance, one objective at least was achieved: Minehead did become a popular resort and still is today. In spite of this, when the Ministry of Transport began axing lines following the publication of the Beeching Plan in 1963, the Minehead line was one of the victims, scheduled for closure in January 1971. Even before closure had been completed, the West

Somerset Railway Association had been formed to attempt to reopen the line as a private steam railway. It was to be a long struggle, with a first modest section between Minehead and Blue Anchor opened in 1976 and extended to Bishop's Lydeard in 1979. Trains can again run to the junction at Norton Fitzwarren, but Bishop's Lydeard remains the normal terminal for passenger trains. Few lines have had a more chequered history, but today the West Somerset is a success story. A company run by fifty paid staff and an impressive army of 900 volunteers. And this was to be my exercise in nostalgia. I did the whole journey in both directions, but to get the real flavour of a seaside line you want to try and recapture the joy of going to the seaside, not the glum day when you had to return home to go back to school. So my journey begins at Bishop's Lydeard, where what was once a modest village halt has become an important terminus.

You can't really recreate the feeling of adventure you had as a small boy, clutching a bucket and spade. Did anyone ever really take a bucket and spade with them? I don't think I ever did, but somehow it's an idea you carry with you through the years. But for a steam enthusiast a trip has its own special sense of excitement and anticipation: which of the locomotives will appear to head our train? It might be anything from a 'foreigner' from the Somerset & Dorset Junction Railway, a very handsome 2-8-0, one of a class designed by Sir Henry Fowler right back in 1914, or perhaps a more modest GWR tank engine. While I was waiting I called in at the little museum.

I have a great fondness for these small railway museums. So many modern museums seem to find it essential to organise everything and rather bossily tell you what you should be looking at and how you should view it. The West Somerset have just collected lots of different things together and slotted them

in wherever there was space. The prize exhibit is a GWR sleeping car of 1897, and very comfortable it looked too: you got a proper bedroom for your money. There's also a big model railway, which doesn't stick slavishly to the local brand, but has Southern trains running from time to time. Purists no doubt would object, but not me. After spending some time chatting, it was time to join the real thing and find out what was to be our beast of burden for the day. It did not disappoint. Even at a distance, it was impossible to miss the glint of sunshine off the polished brass at the tope of the chimney: whatever it was it was going to be ex-GWR. As it got close, all was revealed. It was No. 4160, a 2-6-2T, one of the class first designed by that great engineer George Jackson Churchward and popularly known as 'Large Prairies'.

Setting off with the familiar short panting puffs of an engine getting under way, everything settles down and it's clear that the start is on an uphill gradient. It can't have been easy planning this route. A glance at the Ordnance Survey map shows a complex web of contour lines, representing a bewildering landscape of hills and hollows. So it comes as no great surprise to find oneself passing under a high stone road bridge before disappearing into a cutting soon to be followed by a low embankment: a combination to be repeated again within the next mile. Cuttings have their own appeal. You get a little geology lesson as the underlying red sandstone peeps through the surface soil and they are a good habitat for wild flowers to brighten the journey, from the bright yellow of buttercups to the shocking pink of ragged robin. Then, when you emerge onto a bank you get the wider vista.

This is the sort of landscape that is often described as typically English even if, for people like myself brought up in the north of England, it is very far from typical. This is a countryside that really earns the clichéd description of hills as being rolling, but here they really do look like the green sea swell of the sea. Neat little fields alternate with patches of woodland, some of which at this time of the year were still carpeted with bluebells. Much of the farmland is pasture. We pass a field of disinterested cows that mostly ignore the busily working engine chuffing past them. One animal raises its head to take a look, decides that it is far less interesting than grass and resumes its munching with the rest. Only sheep seem to get perturbed, dashing away from the fence near the line until they have reached the rest of the flock. Occasionally we pass newly harrowed fields which reveal the startling red earth that is such a feature of this part of the world.

The first stop is Crowcombe Heathfield, a halt that seems to serve nowhere in particular: there's a scattering of houses, but the village of Crowcombe is more than a mile away. It's a lovely little spot, nestling down against a background of the Quantock Hills, with an attractive little garden. Mrs Irene Horn came here in 1948 to live in the station house with her husband who ran the local signal box. She stayed on through the restoration years, taking over the job of station master until she finally decided to retire at the age of ninety-two, surely winning a prize as the oldest stationmaster ever. From here the fireman has a chance to take things a bit easier for a while as the long climb has come to an end and the engine coasts quietly along. The scenery remains as enchanting as ever, with the Quantocks to the east offering a hint of wildness, while to the west the line continues to meander through rich farmland. Down in the valley there is an occasional glimpse of water, as the little trickle that started with us on our journey becomes a substantial stream, big enough to be given a name – the Donford Stream. It might not be even big enough to qualify as a river, but in cutting its way through the hills it provided a line for the railway engineers to follow. Even then it was never easy and the line had to be cut into the hillside, and the next stop, Stogumber, finds itself on the opposite side of the valley from the village it is meant to serve.

So far this has been single line working and now there is a wait at Williton to exchange tokens with the train from Minehead. On this short passing loop you can see how far apart the present tracks are: this is a station built originally for the broad gauge. It seemed a good opportunity to visit the buffet car and who could resist a bottle of Steamer beer, brewed by the Cotleigh brewery and featuring one of the West Somerset's own locomotives, *Odney Manor*? Not me. It's not always a good way to buy your beer by choosing the most attractive label, but it seemed to me that if they had enough sense to feature a locomotive, they probably had enough taste to produce a good brew as well. I wasn't wrong. The next question was – what will be coming the other way? If locomotives can be said to have voices then we've been in the company of a tenor. The new arrival was definitely a bass-baritone. This was obviously something on the grand scale, and hoping for a good shot I leaned out of the carriage window, camera at the ready – and not for the first time in my life I was presented with a fine view of an engine approaching tender first. By the time I'd got my head out of the way, it was past me, but it was one of the two Manors, so I toasted it with my Manor beer.

The line now runs out across the widening valley and there's a first brief glimpse of the sea, but no one is tempted to stop the train for the request halt at Doniford so we trundle on into Watchet past the harbour, now full of yachts and cruisers; the days when vessels laden with coal from South Wales have long since passed away. That once mighty industry just across the Bristol Channel did not die: it was killed off by the Thatcher administration. Now you can see ships bringing coal down to Avonmouth, coal from around the world. Apparently it makes sense. It is a change that affected the lives of thousands of miners, and although it is not of the same level of importance, it is also a change that has had its effect on the steam engines of Great Britain. In its day, South Wales was a great producer of high quality steam coal. Getting anything of the same quality these days is becoming increasingly difficult. I remember one of my trips on the VIC32 (chapter 13) when, judging by the acrid smoke, we could have been burning old rubber tyres not coal.

Up to now, station buildings have been conventionally arranged, lined up alongside the rails and platforms. Here they are at right angles to the track, reflecting the fact that this was once the end of the line. So now we are moving out onto the old Minehead Railway, with a stutter of little stops between here and the terminus. The next station

beside the sea is Blue Anchor, but nature has inconveniently left a large hill in between the two spots, which are a mere 3 miles apart to any crow that happens to be flying that way but twice as far by rail – and the company even managed to squeeze in an extra station along the way. But when Blue Anchor does arrive, the real seaside finally appears, a great expanse of sandy beach and shingle. Children fishing in rock pools stop, look up and wave – which is what small children always do when they see a steam train. Perhaps they were all brought up on *Thomas the Tank Engine*.

Now the route stays close to the shoreline, with just one stop at Dunster, with its castle on the hilltop above the village. It always seems to us to be rather romantic to perch a castle on the top of a hill, but where else would you put it if you were serious about using it as a

The 'small boiler' Mogul locomotive beside the seaside on the West Somerset Railway. (West Somerset Railway)

defence against attack? It's a very modest station but it did boast its very own goods shed. In its day it was a versatile little place which, according to the *Clearing House Handbook* for 1904, could cope with everything from livestock to gentlemen's carriages. Now there is just a gentle run in towards Minehead, passing a long rake of goods wagons to one side and a pair of supermarkets to the other. When they built the station they clearly anticipated huge crowds descending on Minehead for the platform seems to go on forever – said to be the longest in the country. Did any train ever really stretch out this long – even in the days when crowds appeared in droves to stay at Billy Butlin's Holiday Camp? At least when you leave the station you can see that the railway did exactly what it started out to do – it created a successful resort, with a cluster of Victorian hotels right outside the station – which perhaps explains why there are no waiting rooms. You could stay in your comfortable hotel until it was time to leave.

There was just one thing to do now. Walk out from the station, and across the road to the bay – even if I hadn't brought a bucket and spade.

The train was not the only way of getting to the seaside in former days. Paddle steamers did a splendid trade in taking people out of crowded cities to enjoy the sea airs. It all started on the Clyde, when a tiny steamer, *Comet,* with a sail hung from its tall funnel– can't trust these new-fangled machines – took passengers from Glasgow to Helensburgh. She was only the first of many, many Clyde steamers and one of them, PS *Waverley*, is now the world's only surviving sea-going paddle steamer. She is still based on the Clyde but now makes regular trips all round the British coast. I joined her for a seaside special, a trip to Ilfracombe in Devon that started in Somerset at Clevedon.

Paddle steamers were busy in the Bristol Channel well into the twentieth

The West Somerset Railway has a fine collection of GWR locomotives and rolling stock: this train is hauled by *Osney Manor*. (West Somerset Railway)

century and piers were built as much to provide a safe deep-water mooring for the steamers as it was to give holidaymakers a chance to stroll out to sea without getting wet feet. Some piers are grand, with all kinds of amusements at the end, but Clevedon is not like that. This is a lovely, delicate pier, its ironwork like filigree. I

This little train isn't actually going anywhere, but it is a charmingly appropriate way to provide flower boxes for the platform at Bishops Lydeard on the West Somerset. (Anthony Burton)

The PS *Waverley*, the last sea-going paddle steamer in the world, on a sunny excursion cruise down the south coast. (Waverley Excursions)

joined friends and the rest of the crowd making their way aboard for what was more than just an ordinary cruise – this was a jazz cruise, timed to coincide with the Ilfracombe Jazz Festival. Among the passengers was an old friend, Mike Cooper, trombonist and band leader and a man of what might tactfully be called considerable girth. It was one of his band who arranged for an announcement to be made over the ship's PA system: 'Would passenger Cooper please stay in the middle of the ship – we don't want to tip over.'

The scenery along the coastline of the Bristol Channel may be fine, but no trip aboard *Waverley*, and there have been many of them over the years, would be even acceptable without a pilgrimage below decks to see the engine at work. It was early in the twentieth century that a captain of the Caledonian Company realised that when he took visitors into the engine room they were hypnotised by the motion of the mighty engine. He decided that all visitors would be equally enchanted, given the chance, so he decided that in future steamers should be built with open engine rooms and walkways to the side for passengers. The idea was an immense success and thanks to the good captain we can all enjoy watching the *Waverley* engine go through its paces.

This is a triple expansion engine of immense size: 24 inch high pressure cylinder, 39 inch intermediate and 62 inch low pressure, together generating an impressive 2,100 indicated horsepower. What is so enthralling is the sight of great masses of steel, moving in elegant curves in perfect harmony. The piston rods from the horizontal cylinders perform an intricate dance to drive the massive crankshaft that turns the paddles. I've rather lost count of how many times I've travelled on this wonderful vessel, but every time I come down to see the engines they seem as imposing as they did on my first trip – and that was over thirty years ago.

We puffed on our way to Ilfracombe on a fine, clear day, enjoying a different view of the coastline – it's not often you get to see it from the seaward side. Everything was set for a wonderful day but, alas, Ilfracombe itself did not really live up to expectations. The town had a faintly tawdry air, but we trooped ashore and made for the first pub offering live jazz. The music wasn't great but the beer was worse – jazz and a pint should be a perfect combination but of the four

of us sat round the table not one could actually drain a glass. We did find another pub, with better music and beer that was actually drinkable. We mentioned our previous experience – ah, he said, you must have gone to the – and I have long since forgotten the name of the pub, which is just as well as it might prevent a libel suit.

The day had been redeemed, and there was always the return journey to look forward to. Off we sailed into the dusk and down in the bar Mike and his men played to a cheery and, admittedly by now, rather beery crowd of enthusiasts. I shall go on *Waverley* again no doubt, but not, I think, to Ilfracombe.

One of the greatest attractions on *Waverley* is the engine room where passengers can see the magnificent triple expansion engine at work. (Waverley Excursions)

Chapter 13

Puffer Passage

Often in my travels I had felt I was renewing an old friendship and this was never more true than when joining Nick Walker in Scotland on the *VIC 32*. It is not the most glamorous name for a ship, and when spelt out as Victualling Inshore Coaster No. 32 it sounds even less exciting.

The VICs were a series of vessels used in the Second World War to provision the fleet off the Scottish coast, and for their design the Admiralty turned to a proven formula. These ships were no more than Clyde puffers taken out of civilian life and put into uniform, like so many others in those years. Few craft have aroused more affection than these sturdy workers of Scotland's west coast. The special feeling came, in large part, from Neil Munro's comic tales of one particular puffer, *The Vital Spark*. Here is skipper Para Handy's own view of the ship: 'If you never saw the *Fital Spark*, she is all hold, with the boiler behind, four men and a derrick and a water-butt and a pan loaf in the fo'c'sle. Oh man! she was the beauty! She was chust sublime!'

That is a fair description of a puffer. She is a tough little go-anywhere coastal steamer, flat-bottomed so that she can be beached if there is no pier. In the bows are the steam winch, the derrick and the fo'c'sle for the crew. There is a cavernous hole beneath hatches, and in the stern is the engine room, the funnel rising inconveniently in front of the wheelhouse. The skipper's cabin completes the assembly. No one, other than Para Handy, has ever spoken of a puffer as a glamorous vessel – workmanlike, certainly, full of character, without a doubt; but not glamorous. No one, other than Para Handy, has described a puffer as anything but a fine little cargo steamer,

doing sterling work serving the scattered communities of the islands and long sea lochs around the mouth of the Clyde. But Para Handy had visions of grandeur for his charge: 'She should be carryin' nothing but gentry for passengers, or nice genteel luggage for the shooting-lodges.' No one took such a vision seriously – until Nick and Rachel Walker found the *VIC 32*.

Nick Walker has been involved with boats all his life but, much as he enjoyed life in a yard on the Grand Union Canal, he hankered to own a real sea-going vessel. Various forays to look at Baltic traders came to nothing, each vessel proving more derelict and less seaworthy than the last. Then, in the autumn of 1975, Nick and Rachel decided to give it one more go and headed north to Newcastle, where a pilot cutter in allegedly superb condition awaited inspection. It proved to be another failure and they left for home vowing again to abandon their pursuit of the impossible. They made an overnight stop in Whitby and the next morning, on the way out of town, they saw a puffer moored at the Whitehall Shipyard Wharf. It is a mystery why, having rejected a succession of wooden sailing ships, they should suddenly become enchanted by an elderly, rusting cargo steamer. They stopped, they looked and were not unduly impressed but, talking it over under the benign influence of several pints of Messrs Cameron's bitter, the rust began to seem less troublesome, the scale less daunting.

A second tour of inspection proved their optimism was not ill-founded. The *VIC 32* was filthy and neglected, but she had been cared for in the past. Down in the gloom of the engine room, muck was scraped away to reveal the engine, well coated with protective grease. The

Walkers thought the old vessel worth preserving. They pumped out the hold and, although no one could pretend that she was in perfect condition, she seemed reasonably sound. My theory is that the puffer may be a good Scottish design, but *VIC 32* owes her survival to having been built in Yorkshire.

Renovation began and the great day arrived when steam was to be raised. The beginning was not propitious as the engine room began to fill with thick clouds of smoke. It was a while before anyone found that interesting device, the funnel damper, which closes off the funnel to keep the furnace banked down overnight. After that, life was more comfortable, and work began preparing the *VIC* for her new career. The days of carrying tins of baked beans to Her Majesty's Navy were over; she was now to become a passenger steamer. It would have been the easiest thing in the world to get this wrong, to destroy the essential nature of the vessel. I remember my apprehension when I went to join the ship in the summer of 1980. Pip and I had taken the Glasgow–Campbeltown bus, and as we came down Loch Fyne towards Tarbert I looked for the first sign of the vessel. We rounded a corner and there was the harbour and tied to the quay the puffer, a thin wisp of smoke straggling from the funnel. It was a moment of pure pleasure because she was exactly what I had hoped for but hardly dared expect. She was a true puffer from stem to stern.

It is no easy matter to change a cargo vessel into a passenger vessel, while keeping its character but providing comfort. Outwardly the changes were minimal. The hatches were raised and glass set into the side supports to provide light. The hold was divided by a new deck, forming a large saloon, a galley and the captain's cabin. Beneath that are two bathrooms and six passenger cabins – comfort and character combined. I was an instant *VIC* addict. After that first visit

my wife and I came back again and again, and in the summer of '86 I joined the ship once more, heading towards the west coast of Scotland.

The *VIC 32* offers a variety of routes for holidaymakers, mostly around the traditional puffer grounds off the mouth of the Clyde, but also through the Caledonian Canal. This time I joined her at the end of a Caledonian cruise to help crew her back to her home port of Crinan. It is, or should be, a gloriously scenic journey out from under the shadow of Ben Nevis and down between the mainland and the islands of Mull and Jura. It was something to anticipate with pleasure, but first there were old acquaintances to renew. Times and personnel had changed. Rachel, with two young children to look after, was no longer on board as head chef, her place having been taken by Caroline, and there was a new engineer, Paul. Nick was still there, and the success of the *VIC* lies in his personality as much as that of his ship.

Californians take pride in having invented the condition known as 'laid back'. Nick could give them a few lessons. I have never known him panic. He showed only the mildest concern on a previous occasion when we were sailing in the PTC's dinghy in a howling gale off Arran with water coming up through the centreboard rather faster than I was able to bale it out. I have never seen him other than affable with even the most cantankerous of passengers, and I marvel at the way he lets total strangers take over important tasks around the vessel which is his livelihood. Admittedly, he is not likely to leave a novice alone at the helm, but how many owners would let passengers anywhere near the wheel? It was good to be back.

Weather permitting, the plan was to make the run down to Crinan on the Saturday. The weather permitted but did not please. It can best be described in the lowland Scots phrase *'gey dreich'* The word *dreich* uttered in good round

Scots conjures up all the misery of grey, damp, cheerless days when the weather seems to be seeping into the centre of your body. The clouds were low and dark, Ben Nevis had disappeared and the coastguard's reports were of fog banks out to sea. But the wind was light and the sea calm, so we decided to go. The other volunteers helping the regular crew were a party from the Worth Valley Railway. They say railway buffs care for nothing that does not move on rails – single-track minds – but these were dedicated puffer enthusiasts. It was soon obvious that there would be a queue for the privilege of shovelling coal in the engine room, so I volunteered for the wheelhouse and what was to prove an unusually interesting day at the helm.

Out through the sea lock and on to the waters of Loch Linnhe we went, and life began to look more hopeful. Visibility was good and the rain was easing, though at the horizon sea and sky seemed joined in a seamless blanket of grey. It was a monochrome world that surrounded us, composed of nothing but shades of grey: light for sea and sky, darker colours marking the land. But there was not a great deal of time to view the scenery.

Paul had been welding new metal on to the platform immediately forward of the wheelhouse, and no one had found out how much this had affected the compass. All compasses point more or less to magnetic north, but there are variations depending on local conditions, and these are shown on the Admiralty charts. Further differences affect each compass on each vessel, and there will be a different variation for each point of the compass. In other words the variation when the vessel is heading south can be different from that when heading east. If, as seemed probable, we were going to hit fog, we were going to need to steer by compass. It was important to know the result of the welding.

Many years ago I was trained as a navigator and I rather enjoy using old skills, even if my techniques have become rusty. The simplest way to correct the compass is to take transit bearings. You locate two prominent landmarks – say a lighthouse and a radio mast – and you peer at them over a prism mounted on the rim of the compass, so that when they are in line you can read off the compass mark which shows in the prism. Suppose it reads 270°, you then go back to your charts to find out what the true magnetic bearing is. If that comes out at 268°, you know that you have a 2° error when the compass is pointing west. It was, to say the least, interesting to discover that the new metalwork had produced a change of 7°; in other words, had we been foolish enough to believe the compass without testing it, we should have ended our journey about eight miles from where we intended, not in Crinan Basin but halfway up a mountain. We had scarcely established the variation before the weather closed in and landmarks disappeared from view.

Steering is a relaxed affair when you do have landmarks to steer by. Travelling down Loch Linnhe you need do little more than keep the land equidistant on either side and point the bows down the middle. Steering by compass is far more tiring, for you are concentrating on just the one thing – a needle pointing at a number which is the heading you should be keeping. The puffer seems to have its own views on where it should go. You nonchalantly hold the wheel in one hand, watching as the compass rose indicates a steady, untroubled progress. Then, for no apparent reason, it takes off to port or starboard, swinging through 10° before you can blink. You bring it back, but it refuses to accept your ruling and heads off on another wayward course. Just when you are becoming exasperated, the *VIC* decides that fun and games time is over and settles back to conformity. You sigh in relief, look up at last and all you can see is the image of the compass rose fixed on your brain.

Ten miles down Loch Linnhe, the channel is nipped by a pincer of land to form the Corran Narrows. We were approaching this point at our maximum speed of six knots, which was achieved only by keeping the furnace fed steadily to produce a boiler pressure of around 100 psi, just below the blow-off point. We were likely to need all the power we could get, because the rising water was streaming up through the narrows, creating a bubbling, whirling tidal rip. Looking out from the wheelhouse, I could see a likely approach, an area of slack water bounded by the streaks and bubbles of the faster current. We were lucky: this was the period of gentle neap tides; had the powerful spring tides been running we would not have got through. Even so, the vessel was thrown from side to side, and I had to spin the wheel first one way then the other to keep us in the centre of the gap.

As we passed the narrows, the clouds began to lift and the sun imparted a gunmetal sheen to the waves. Other vessels emerged from the murk, including a handsome wooden sailing boat with traditional gaff rig. For a while there was time to enjoy the scenery and I handed over the wheel as we chugged past Mull, its peaks still lost in the clouds. At least we could now distinguish the soft browns and greens of the lower slopes. Shuna Island appeared, its rocky shoreline looking inhospitable. But there is a farm on the island, the ideal spot for those who welcome solitude. There was once a castle here, visible among the trees as a ruin, and a second castle perches on its own rocky islet in the bay.

The breaks in the fog gave a chance to look around, and what a lot there was to see, sliding down between the islands. You wonder who could ever have chosen these small patches of ground off the western coast for their homes, but choose them they did. There are lime-kilns on an island, but the stone could not have come from anywhere nearer than Cumberland.

Someone thought it worth the trouble to produce the lime to help green these rocky islets. Belnahua was quarried, and through the binoculars I could make out the remains of buildings and the rusting shells of steam engines which once worked here. What a busy trade there once was, and no doubt vessels such as the *VIC* played their part. This is only a part of the history, for near the crumbling engines you will find ancient burial mounds. There are islands with no occupants but grazing sheep and others which support communities of fishermen. It is a rich and varied world on the west coast of Scotland, which maintains its identity in spite of a tendency in the twentieth century towards dull conformity.

I was back at the wheel just as we reached the next fog bank. It was to stay with us all the way to Crinan, which gave food for thought, as our passage lay through some narrow gaps between islands. There are times when a knowledge of history can be a disadvantage, for I was reminded that Britain's first commercial steamer, the *Comet*, worked these waters and foundered in 1820 at just this spot off Craignish Point. Nick was setting the course, peering into the radar and, like me, hoping that our compass variation had been accurately calculated. In the event we came right in through the middle of the gap, the tidal race gave us a mild buffeting and we were through, heading straight on until the reassuring white shape of the Crinan Hotel appeared through the mist. Then we had simply to manoeuvre through the lock and out into the basin, where we tied up alongside a sister ship, *Auld Reekie*, one of the other select company of coal-fired puffers. She was a famous film star in her day, but, like many of her human equivalents, was now somewhat faded and looking for a face lift.

One cannot complain about lack of variety on the puffer. After a long passage down the west coast we were faced by

The Clyde puffer VIC32 almost lost among the trees on the Crinan Canal. (David Hawson)

a short passage in terms of distance, a mere nine miles, but long in terms of time. We were to travel down the Crinan Canal, a short cut across a narrow neck of land which saves a 132-mile trip round the Mull of Kintyre. It looks alarmingly narrow, but the official records say it is designed for craft up to 88 feet long by 20 feet beam. The *VIC 32* is a comparatively modest 70 feet by 18 feet so in theory there was room to spare – which just goes to show how misleading figures can be. Progress was painfully slow. I had volunteered as lock-wheeler, going ahead of the ship to set the locks – thirteen between the two basins, and all but the entry lock worked by hand. As the actual route is narrow and twisting, and as water depth is not all it should be, I had no problems keeping ahead of the steamer. The only problems I did have were those of muscle power as I heaved and shoved

at the massive lock gates. I was rewarded by the astonishing sight of what looked to be an enormous vessel in the tiny canal. The waterway was keeping me in a fine old sweat and was having a similar effect, but for different reasons, on Nick in the wheelhouse. He was concentrating on keeping the vessel in the channel. The engine room crew, however, were taking it easy. As the ship travelled forward at about two knots, the firing rate was down to a nonchalant shovelful at irregular intervals.

The grey morning gave way to a sunny afternoon and as the sun came out so did the tourists. The canal often runs close to the road, and motorists confronted by what appears to be a steamer in a field turn and stare, forgetting such mundane matters as avoiding ditches and other motorists. The owners of a German yacht coming down a lock stared in amazement.

'Was is das?' they demanded. *'Das ist ein Puffer'* I replied, thereby exhausting my German vocabulary.

Spectators are often keen to help. I had marched on to set a series of locks and found a mini-flotilla of yachts and cruisers descending the flight. I asked them to leave the bottom gates open as they went down, which would mean we could go straight into the locks on the way up. They obliged, but I had not made allowance for the helpful spectators who, not being party to the arrangement, closed all of them. When that happens leakage is going to let water in, so I had all the locks to empty and all the gates to shove open again all the way back. I had a pleasant morning on the bank and back on board they were probably pleased to have one less body as a party of schoolchildren had joined for the day and were having a splendid time. Also on board were Rachel, the children and another old friend, Rupert the red setter.

Rupert was always one of the ship's characters: a dog with an astonishingly well-controlled bladder, who was not perturbed by the calls of nature no matter how long the voyage between ports. He was also a true sailor for when we reached land he was off with wagging tail and a gleam in his eye. Heaven alone knows how many crossbred setters there are around the Clyde estuary. One blast of the steam whistle, however, brought him loping back down pier or quay. And if a dog can be said to have a self-satisfied smirk, Rupert had on those occasions.

Much of the pleasure of travel on the Crinan Canal is the pleasure of travel on any canal. Progress is stately, allowing time to contemplate the works of man and those of nature. Of the former, the canal provides the main interest: cut from the solid rock at the Crinan end, in what must have been a mighty labour, supplied with swing bridges with attendant bridgekeeper's cottages and, most important, the locks. It was begun at the height of the canal mania years, in 1793,

when it was believed that all canals would return vast profits to investors. Optimism was short-lived. The Crinan was underfinanced from the very beginning, and the slow progress of the *VIC 32* at the western end, at times scraping the bottom of the canal, can be traced back to those days. The cash ran out and instead of being dug to a depth of fifteen feet as planned, the canal was reduced at the western end to ten feet. It was never practical or profitable, but is scenically splendid.

Rough hillsides and glimpses of the sea mark the passage. Closer at hand a statuesque heron watched with irritation the approach of a noisy steamer. The heron is the photographer's *bête noir*. You stare down the viewfinder as you edge closer and as you arrive at the perfect moment to click the shutter, it flies off, to land a little farther along and you begin the infuriating process again. Ahead of the vessel the weeds waved sinuously in the water, then dipped and sank, dragged down by the sucking of the propellor. The water was brown and peaty, which puts me in mind of the smell of peat smoke, which in turn suggests the flavour of malt whisky – and that, sooner or later, will bring a visit to the ship's excellent selection of malts. There is still a wonderful richness and variety to enjoy in Scotland, though less than there used to be, as the sight of a defunct distillery at Lochgilphead sadly reminded me.

Ardrishaig marks the easterly end of the canal and our release from its restrictions. The plan for the week was to head down Loch Fyne and visit the sea lochs and the islands of Bute, Great Cumbrae and Arran – the whole to be interspersed with the splendid meals which were a feature of our puffer holidays. There is a wonderful sense of calm about puffing out to sea, with none of the unpleasant vibration and sickly smell which marks the diesel engine. There is no noise, except for the steady slap of water; nothing to disturb idle deckhands, apart from the occasional billow of smoke when the

The author (left) and a fellow enthusiast, Wayne Smith, enjoying a day stoking in the VIC32 engine room. (Jane Smith)

wind blows from the stern to the bows. This is not a matter of concern to the gang below decks, shovelling away in the engine room, an isolated world of moving machinery and heat. A series of iron-runged ladders leads down to this dark constricted space. At the forward end is the big vertical boiler, with coal bunkers on either side. You can feed the boiler directly only from the starboard bunker so, on occasion, coal has to be moved across by the shovelful from port to starboard. One of the less popular jobs is ashing out, when the ash is shovelled into buckets which are hauled up to the deck and their contents chucked overboard. Aft of the boiler is the engine, which seems to have three cylinders, but has only two. It is a thorough-going hybrid. There is a high-pressure cylinder with a piston valve alongside – the 'third cylinder' – and a low-pressure cylinder fitted with a slide valve. Steam from the low-pressure cylinder is condensed in a separate condenser, as in a beam engine. The slurping you hear is sea water being pumped around the condenser to cool it,

and the condensed water is pumped back as feed water to the boiler. Below the busy piston is the crank taking the drive to the propeller shaft. It is a joy to watch, though boiler duty does not provide much leisure time.

The *VIC 32* is not a speedboat. She chuffs along at a steady six knots or so and the secret of stoking is to keep things steady, 'a little and often' being the golden rule. I recall a previous trip when I had been taking things a little too easy and pressure had dropped ten pounds or so below the optimum. A call down the speaking tube from the bridge told me that we were approaching a measured mile and everyone wanted to know just how fast we could go. Would I please see that the needle of the pressure gauge stayed firmly fixed just below blow-off point? This meant opening the vent of the ashbox to allow the maximum draught of air through the grate, shovelling a great deal of coal around the box and raking furiously to prevent clinker forming. All this has to be done in such a constricted space that you have to remember to keep your fingers inside the shovel handle or you crack your knuckles on the engine guard on the back swing. We had a full head of steam when we reached the mile and a full head of steam all down it. We made just over six knots, the same as always. The only difference was in me – I was about half a stone lighter. Such are the joys of life in the engine room, and we still come back for more.

More conventional pleasures were the grandeur of the Highland scenery and the variety of our stopping places. Loch Riddon provides the most peaceful of settings, moored up next to a Scottish baronial lodge with the heathered hillside rising above the loch. Rothesay on Bute is a total contrast, a popular seaside resort where once the paddle steamers of the Clyde deposited thousands of Glaswegians for a day's jollification. Now Rothesay is like the old lady at the corner table in a once-fashionable hotel,

who muses over an interesting past while trying to keep up appearances in the present. The town's Victorian villas, topped with spectacular wrought-iron crowns, turn out on closer inspection to be like the old lady, somewhat the worse for wear beneath the paintwork. The town can, however, boast a castle, an entertaining little museum and an amazing Gents on the pier.

Altogether more genteel is Millport on Great Cumbrae, where my wife and I hired a tandem and completed the circuit of the island in one hour. The most dramatic island is Arran with its mountainous spine which in profile takes on the shape of a sleeping, helmeted warrior. The pier at Lochranza is not all it should be, and it is an extraordinary sensation to stand on a massive wooden pier of apparent solidity and feel the entire structure sway. It did not seem a good idea to stay for long.

Rev. Teddy Boston on his traction engine, *Fiery Elias*, watching *Pixie* being loaded back onto the track of the Cadeby Light Railway. (Teddy Boston)

Between the stops come the sea passages, sometimes enlivened by encounters with other craft. We met the Ardrishaig Sailing School and watched the learners practising the difficult but essential art of righting a capsized dinghy. The sun may have been shining but the water looked cold and there were few signs of pleasure among the damp sailors. We also met the Royal Navy in the shape of a frigate out on exercises, with a Nimrod circling overhead. And we renewed acquaintance with the Maids of Bute.

There is a tricky narrow channel between the Kyles of Bute and the mainland and prominent on the island are two rocks painted in gaudy colours. These are the Maids, though it is a mystery why these shapeless hunks of rock should be thought maidenly. According to the Para Handy tales, a captain of the *Inverary Castle* was put in mind of 'the two MacFadyen Gyurls', and it was Para Handy who set out with two pots of paint to decorate the rocks and christen them Elizabeth and Mary. Be that as it may, the rocks are still regularly painted, though we felt as we puffed by that they lacked attention.

The steamer has many advantages over lesser craft, for steam is a versatile source of power. It can be used to generate electricity and to turn the winch for launching and recovering the wooden skiff. No steamer would be complete without its whistle, but the *VIC 32* has gone one or seven better, for it is equipped with a calliope. It has a limited musical range of one octave, with no sharps or flats, but it can produce a spirited if not entirely accurate rendition of *Blue Bells of Scotland*. Steam can also be put to other unconventional uses. At Loch Riddon we made up a cockling party in which steam was to play its part.

Here are the official instructions for steam cockling. First, put on large boots and make your way down to the muddy shoreline. Locate an appropriate

implement among the flotsam and jetsam – a broken cup is ideal but a big scallop shell is acceptable. To take an implement with you is not the done thing. Implement collected, select a piece of shore and jump in the air, landing firmly on flat feet. This alarms lurking cockles, which send up bubbles of air. Dig under the blowhole and there is your cockle. Second, having filled your bucket, return at a modest speed to your puffer, collecting available driftwood as you go. Back on board, feed the wood into the boiler.

Wash the cockles thoroughly and half fill the bucket with water. Attach a steam lance to the steam supply, turn on the steam and stick the lance in the bucket for precisely three minutes. Empty the water from the bucket, remove cockles from shells and dowse them in vinegar and paprika. Eat the cockles, which are guaranteed to taste better than cockles ever tasted before.

The highlight of the steam week was the setting up of the unique steam gramophone. I have never seen another such machine so I cannot make comparisons, but I am fairly certain that no other gramophone has a larger power unit as the steam comes from the ship's boiler. A pressure of 100psi is a trifle excessive for a gramophone, so a reduction valve is brought in to bring it down to around 30psi. The steam is fed to a small, tabletop engine which drives one of the old-style 78rpm gramophones, which before the advent of steam had to be cranked by hand. Steam automation has removed that hardship. To be honest, it has not been perfected, as the turntable currently revolves at about 73rpm, though, given the age of the records, the slight difference in sound is not easily detected.

We listened to the great Fats Waller and lesser artistes who performed such appropriate numbers as, *He played his ukelele while the ship went down*. Further developments are being planned. It seems a waste to allow exhaust steam to pass up the copper pipe and escape; perhaps if we fed it into a bucket of soapy water we could establish the world's first combined gramophone and laundry.

The great appeal of life on the *VIC 32* is that it combines a serious purpose with good fun. Clyde puffers were splendid examples of a whole class of small working steamers which plied the coast of Britain. Very few such craft are left and her preservation as a working vessel is as important as the preservation of any great Victorian beam engine or classic locomotive. She could be preserved in a museum and taken out for the occasional trip. Instead, she is travelling regularly over the routes she traded for many years. She is providing immense pleasure for a great many people; not just those lucky enough to travel on her, but all who come to watch her entering and leaving harbour, who come on board to peer down into the engine room and savour the life of the ship for a few minutes. She is a supreme example of the truth that preservation need not be solemn. And if steam cockling and the steam gramophone seem eccentric, I see nothing wrong with that.

Chapter 14

A Farewell to Steam

I have always been attracted to what some regard as eccentricities. Many call slightly mad those who become passionate about an old steam engine. They find quirky, if not reprehensible, the notion of people spending time and money on bringing old machines back to life. Could you not do something more useful they demand, though I seldom notice them at the helm of worthier causes. I warm to those who work at restoration not just for fun, but often at considerable expense of time and cash. It gives much harmless pleasure to many other than themselves.

When this book was first mooted, I had an image of one man in one place who seemed to epitomise everything I found appealing in the world of steam. That man was the Reverend E. R. Boston, Vicar of Cadeby. He died in 1986, but a book about a passion for steam would not be complete without a few words about Teddy Boston and the Cadeby Light Railway.

Cadeby is a quiet little village near Market Bosworth. Its centrepiece is the parish church, surrounded by a well-kept graveyard. If you had visited there on certain Saturday afternoons, knowing no more than this, you might have been surprised. As you walked around the church, you would have heard the shrill cry of a steam whistle and seen a plume of smoke and steam above the trees. Around the corner of the rectory would come *Pixie,* a narrow-gauge Bagnell of 1919, with the vicar at the controls. Many people have model railways, a few even have miniature-gauge railways, but this is no toy and no miniature. *Pixie* had a working life as an industrial engine. Her little line is short but it twists and bends through the trees behind the house, and many a railway buff first took the

controls of a working engine on this short track. That, however, is only a part of the Cadeby story.

The house shouts Teddy's love of railways. There is scarcely a space free of models and pictures and railway signs, and the shelves groan under the weight of railway volumes. There was always someone in the library, usually a visitor free to range through the collection. Outside there was more activity. A shed contains a magnificent model railway layout, devoted to Teddy's favourite line, the GWR. You need half a dozen manipulators of controls to get the best out of this and run a proper schedule. I suppose he started as I did with one clockwork train on an oval track and somehow it just went on from there. Now it is an entire West Country landscape populated by main lines and branch lines, with stations and tunnels, viaducts and bridges, sidings and points. Teddy was just as enthusiastic about the model inside as he was about the real thing outside. He and I also had this in common – our love of steam stretched beyond the world of the railway.

Outside the front door of the rectory, on steam days, you would find his traction engine on the simmer. He never needed an excuse to go off for a jaunt into the country lanes round Cadeby. With Teddy driving and me steering we swooped down impossibly narrow byways, riding high above the surrounding hedges. Oily spray spattered my sweater, and I did not mind. Teddy's old grey cardigan was probably too impregnated with oil for any further intake to make a difference. It was an activity that had no justification except the pure joy of it. That was true of everything in Teddy Boston's world of steam. It was all there because he loved it

– and it was all there to be shared.

I remarked to him once that there seemed to be an extraordinary connection between the Church of England and the steam railway, and he quoted one of the best known lovers of steam, the Reverend W. Awdry, creator of *Thomas the Tank Engine:* 'The steam railway and the Church of England have a lot in common:

they are the best way of getting to a Good Place.' I cannot think of a better epitaph for Teddy Boston. The world is a poorer place without him, for there are not many people who bring a sense of happiness to all they do. Teddy Boston and the Cadeby Light Railway were always meant to have a place in this book. They deserve the last word.

Gazetteer

These are the locations visited and described as they appear in the book: sadly the Cadeby Light Railway has now closed.

1. Waiting for the Train
Didcot Railway Centre
The Station
Didcot
Oxfordshire OX11 7NJ
www.didcotrailwaycentre.org.uk

2. Pumps and Paddles
London Museum of Water and Steam
Green Dragon Lane
Brentford
London TW8 0EN
www.waterandsteam.org.uk

PS *Kingswear Castle*
Kingswear Signal Box
The Square
Kingswear TQ6 0AA
www.paddlesteamerk.co.uk

3. Bluebells and Beams
Kent & East Sussex Railway
Tenterden Town Station
Tenterden
Kent TN30 6HE
www.kesr.org.uk

The British Engineerium
The Droveway
Hove
East Sussex BN3 7QA
www.britishengineerium.org

The Bluebell Railway
Sheffield Park Station
Nr. Uckfield
East Sussex TN22 3QL
www.bluebell-railway.co.uk

4. Red Dragon
Mainline Steam Tours
www.uksteamtours.info

5. Scenery and Slate
The Talyllyn Railway
Wharf Station
Tywyn
Gwynedd LL36 9EY
www.talyllyn.co.uk

The Ffestiniog and Welsh Highland
Railways
Harbour Station
Porthmadog
Gwynedd LL49 9NF
www.festrail.co.uk

The Snowdon Mountain Railway
Llanberis
Gwynedd LL55 4TY
www.snowdonrailway.co.uk

6. Watery Themes
The Battlefield Line Railway
Shackerstone Station
Nr. Market Bosworth
Leicestershire CV13 6NW
www.battlefield-line-railway.co.uk

The Severn Valley Railway
Kidderminster Station
Kidderminster DY10 1QR
www.svr.co.uk

The Nene Valley Railway
Wansford Station
Stibbington
Peterborough PE8 6LR
www.nvr.org.uk

Papplewick Pumping Station
Rigg Lane
Ravenshead
Nottinghamshire NG15 9AJ
www.papplewickpumpingstation.co.uk

7. The Rally
National Traction Engine Trust
4 Church Green East
Redditch
Worcestershire B98 8BT
www.ntet.co.uk

The Great Dorset Steam Fair
Tarrant Hinton
Blandford Forum
Dorset DT11 8HX
www.gdsf.co.uk

8. Moorland Journeys
British Pullman
www.belmond.com/british-pullman-train

The Keighley and Worth Valley
The Railway Station
Haworth
West Yorkshire BD22 8NJ
www.kwvr.co.uk

The North Yorkshire Moors
Pickering Station
Pickering
North Yorkshire YO18 7AJ
www.nymr.co.uk

9. Steam at t'Mill
The Northern Mill Engine Society
Bolton Steam Museum
Mornington Road
Off Chorley Old Road
Bolton BL1 4EU
www.nmes.org

Trencherfield Mill Engine
Wigan Pier Quarter
Heritage Way
Wigan WN3 4EF
www.wigan.gov.uk/resident/museums-
archive/Trencherfield-Mill-engine

Queen Street Mill
Harle Syke
Burnley
Lancashire BB10 2HX
www.burnley.co.uk/visit/culture/queen-
street-mill-textile-museum

St. Mary's Mill
Chalford,
Gloucestershire GL6 8NX
www.stroud-textile.org.uk

10. Hills and Lakes
Lakeside and Haverthwaite Railway
Haverthwaite Station
Nr. Ulverston
Cumbria LA12 8AL
www.lakesiderailway.co.uk

Windermere Steamboat Museum
Rayrigg Road
Windermere
Cumbria LA23 1BN
www.windermerejetty.org

Ravenglass and Eskdale Railway
Ravenglass Station
Cumbria CA18 1SW
www.ravenglass-railway.co.uk

11. Puffer Passage
VIC 32
Puffer Preservation Trust
The Change House
Crinan Ferry
Lochgilphead
Argyll PA31 8QH
www.savethepuffer.co.uk

12. Bucket and Spade
West Somerset Railway
The Railway Station
Minehead TA24 5BG
www.westsomersetrailway.co.uk

PS *Waverley*
Waverley Excursions Ltd.
36 Lancefield Quay
Glasgow G3 8HA
www.waverleyexcursions.co.uk

Index